THE LIFE OF A PSYCHOLOGIST

The Life of a
PSYCHOLOGIST
AN AUTOBIOGRAPHY

by Fritz Heider

UNIVERSITY PRESS OF KANSAS

TO MY SONS
KARL, JOHN, AND STEPHAN

© 1983 by the University Press of Kansas

All rights reserved

Published by the University Press of Kansas (Lawrence, Kansas 66045), which was organized by the Kansas Board of Regents and is operated and funded by Emporia State University, Fort Hays State University, Kansas State University, Pittsburg State University, the University of Kansas, and Wichita State University

Library of Congress Cataloging in Publication Data

Heider, Fritz, 1896-
The life of a psychologist.

Includes index.
1. Heider, Fritz, 1896- . 2. Psychologists—United States—Biography. 3. Psychology—History. I. Title.
BF109.H44A34 1983   150'.92'4 [B]   82-21803
ISBN 0-7006-0232-1

Printed in the United States of America

Contents

List of Illustrations

Preface

I began to write this account of my life because I was invited to contribute a chapter to the series of volumes entitled *A History of Psychology in Autobiography*, now being edited by Professor Gardner Lindzey of the Center for Advanced Study in the Behavioral Sciences in Palo Alto, California. As I started trying to write that chapter, I found myself enjoying this journey to times long past, and I also remembered how I would have liked to be able to read a story of my father's life, but no such biography existed. In the end I decided to begin by reminiscing in a more leisurely way than the chapter I had been asked to write would allow, and to think of my three sons and a few psychologist friends as the principal readers. Then I prepared a shorter version for the *History*.

As time passes, I realize that there will be some readers of this longer narrative who are not psychologists and who, therefore, will not be familiar with all the names that I have mentioned. On that account I will add a little about some of the people who belonged to the fields of psychology and philosophy during my earlier days.

A major background figure was Wilhelm Wundt (1832–1920), whose emphasis was on analyzing experience into "ultimate" elements and determining how these elements combine to give us the world of everyday life. G. E. Müller (1850–1934) followed very much in the Wundtian tradition. E. B. Titchener (1867–1927) was "an Englishman who represented the German psychological tradition in America," to quote E. G. Boring. Boring himself was one of Titchener's students and became a professor at Harvard.

In German-speaking countries, opposition groups arose. Perhaps the most influential was the triad of gestalt psychologists with its center in Berlin. This group consisted of Max Wertheimer (1880–1943), whose 1912 paper marks the beginning of the movement; Kurt Koffka (1886–1941); and Wolfgang Köhler (1887–1967). The work of Franz Brentano (1838–1917) and of Christian von Ehrenfels (1859–1932), especially Ehrenfels's 1890 paper on "form-qualities," helped shape the background of their thinking. Wertheimer, Koffka, and Köhler studied the whole properties of everyday visual experience, believing that those wholes have characteristics that are not to be found in the so-called elements.

Karl Bühler (1879–1963), who taught in Munich and later in Vienna, introduced his own form of gestalt psychology, and there were bitter exchanges between him and the Berlin group over the differences between their two approaches. Vittorio Benussi, whom I had known in Graz, disagreed with the Berlin gestalt psychologists on some of their tenets, but in a less hostile manner. Other European psychologists whom I mention were not involved in these conflicts. Among them were William Stern and Heinz Werner, whom I came to know in Hamburg.

Kurt Lewin (1890–1947), who was in Berlin during my stays there, had moved into studies of action and behavior.

He was probably the émigré of the Nazi period who had the greatest influence on American psychology, both through his own work and through the students who worked with him.

Fritz Heider

Lawrence, Kansas
1981/82

Europe

EARLY YEARS

I was born in Vienna, Austria, in 1896, and when I was half a year old, my parents moved to Graz, which is the capital of the Austrian province of Styria. My father, Moriz, was an architect who worked for the provincial government. This job was very much to his taste, for he was a man of hobbies that he enjoyed as much as he did his work. His office day ended at two o'clock; then he came home for a family dinner, followed by the inevitable Austrian nap. After this, there was time for his personal interests, which included sketching as he wandered about the countryside. Every couple of years he would build a new house for his family, which he and my mother planned together, usually in the same section of Graz. In recent years I have walked through the streets and seen several of these houses that are still standing.

Another of my father's interests was archeology. He had heard the story that somewhere in the region of Graz there were ruins that went back to Roman times. This story caught his imagination, and he began wandering about the hills nearby until he found what he thought would be a likely place to begin to dig. He hired some workmen to help him in the evenings after their regular work hours. They dug together in the darkness, using lights; and this caused talk of ghostly happenings among the more superstitious residents of the neighborhood. Finally my father and the workmen found the remains of a Roman fortress and a small temple. My father donated a number of items from the dig to the museum in Graz, where I have often seen them. There was also a golden ring, with the inscription "When you wear this you will be happy." He liked to tell how he wore it for a year, which was perhaps one of the happiest years of his life. By that time he felt that the ring, also, should go to the museum, and my impression was that he remembered a change in his luck after he gave it up, but he never quite told what happened.

My early youth was a very happy one. I had a brother, Edward, who was two years older than I, with whom I played and wrestled. Our parents often joined in our cheer-

Fritz, Edi, Eugenie, and Moriz Heider toasting the New Year

ful games, and all of us would get to laughing at some silly joke and laugh until we were exhausted. My mother, Eugenie, had been a gifted amateur actress, and she liked to entertain us with strikingly funny take-offs of people we knew. She was full of Viennese vitality and gaiety, and her nickname of "Schnitzel" seemed very much to fit her.

Though I was not quite four years old when the new century began, I remember some earlier incidents and can place these memories by the house in which we lived at the time. I must have been about two years old when I had a flash of insight about having a self, about being a person. It was a kind of ego experience, and the event is clearly connected with the visual memory of the house and the place in the house where it occurred. I was sitting on a little footstool in a sort of nook formed by the door between two rooms. My father was reading or telling a story to my brother, and I felt somehow left out, excluded from what was going on, frustrated. And I remember the awareness that it was *I* who was frustrated. In spite of the sadness at being neglected, the discovery of the self was like an exciting illumination.

Another memory of this time falls into place in history. It was in October 1898, and I was two-thirds of a year past my second birthday. It was dark, and my father was out. My mother and my brother and I were standing in front of our house, waiting for him, when two men rushed by, talking about some terrible event. Soon Father came and, as I only understood later, told the story of the assassination of the Empress Elisabeth.

At the age of six my formal education was supposed to begin, and my parents decided that I should not yet go to school but have a private teacher at home. I have a feeling that they thought of me as an unusually sensitive, high-strung, vulnerable sort of child and decided that I should be protected from the rough life of a regular primary school. A very warm, motherly woman came five days a week and started teaching me the ABCs. I loved her, and I loved all the interesting things that could be done with letters and figures. What impressed me was the simple fact of writing. That one could put down on paper a description of something that had happened, that one could carry that piece of paper around like any other "thing," that even another person could read it and know what had happened—all this seemed very wonderful. And the greatest miracle of all was that one could even make a piece of paper hold events that had never happened—that were mere adventures of fantasy. These were intoxicating thoughts, and I remember clearly how on a certain day I came to understand all these delightful possibilities.

I also acquired very early—maybe when I was seven—a familiarity with painting and sketching. Both my mother and father painted and drew: my mother had even had lessons from the painter Klimt, long before he had become famous. Most of my closer relatives had painting as a hobby, and it seemed quite as natural to play around with a pencil and paints as to learn to walk. I also remember from this early time how I liked to lie on the rug and listen while my mother played the piano. She had big volumes with selections from operas, symphonies, and all sorts of music. Her piano was a constant source of pleasure.

When I was nine years old, my parents sent me to a public school, where there was a kind of preparatory class for children who were to move on to a more advanced school. For some reason I was the only pupil in that class for the first half of the school year. For me the situation was not very different from what I had been used to when I was being taught by a private teacher at home. However, the teacher, a rather crusty, grumpy sort of person, did not see it that way. I still remember one small incident that tells something of the rigid discipline of my early school years: I noticed that he looked at his watch, and I asked him naïvely what time it was. He was suddenly angry, because he saw this as a school situation in which it was sheer impudence for a pupil to ask a teacher the time. But my reaction to his outburst must have made him realize that my question did not come from impudence but from complete ignorance of the customs of the school situation, with its opposition between the status and rank of the teacher and that of a pupil. This ignorance was, of course, a consequence of the well-meant attempt of my parents to shield me from the harsh realities of life in a regular school.

During the second half of the school year, three or four other boys joined the class. I remember only one incident from this time: I found out in some way that one of these boys had lied to me about something. This was a completely new experience for me; it disturbed me greatly and gave me much to think about.

Around the age of nine and ten the generally carefree and cheerful life that I had led came to an abrupt end. Fate dealt me two blows that made me stagger and flounder about for a time before I came to some sort of equilibrium again. First, there was the affair with my eye. My brother and I had little cap pistols. These caps seemed to have remarkable properties, and I decided to experiment to find out more about them. The upshot was that something exploded in my face. Several little pieces of lead became imbedded in my cheeks and forehead, and a few entered my left eye, injuring the retina. My father took me to our doctor right away. He was rather pessimistic about the outlook for the eye. I remember that I had to stay in bed for two weeks, with my eyes covered. I had no pain as I lay there, but I had a dim feeling that something of importance had happened which would influence my whole life. I could not judge whether this would be beneficial or harmful—I only knew that there was something serious about it, though I do not remember that I was unduly worried.

Another event that occurred at about the same time was the cause of much greater immediate anguish and distress. It again had to do with school discipline of that day. When a boy was ten years old, the decision had to be made as to whether he would go to the *Gymnasium,* where Latin and Greek were taught, or to the *Realschule,* which stressed modern languages (English and French), mathematics, and sciences. When my parents asked me which I would prefer, I decided in favor of science and modernity and started out in the *Realschule.* The first days in class were very exciting. I had never before been with thirty or forty boys of my own age, and the possibilities of finding congenial friends seemed limitless. On the second or third day we had a teacher who was full of tricks and jokes and made the boys laugh and shout with glee. Being part of merrymaking like this made me feel at home in this new setting, and I wanted to add my bit. I had just learned to whistle with a special trill. Here seemed the right place to display this new talent of which I felt so proud—it would add to the festive atmosphere. But alas, it did not have the intended effect. At the first whistle, a deadly silence fell over the crowd of boys who had been so joyful, and they looked at me with terror-stricken faces. I had obviously committed a crime. The teacher ordered me to go to the platform and stand there in a corner for the rest of the hour. I had violated a code that was familiar to everyone else, teacher and pupils. As I wandered about during the next recess, I could feel that there was a sort of distance between me and the other boys, who looked at me as though I were something sinister. Life became very difficult.

My parents soon got the whole story out of me, and when they suggested that I leave this school and go to the gymnasium that my brother attended, I was greatly relieved. This gymnasium was not a state school but a private boarding school that also accepted day pupils. It had the reputation of being less difficult than the state schools. My brother had been sent there because he had a hard time with languages. He had somewhat one-sided gifts: he was fascinated with electrical gadgets and that sort of thing, while languages, ancient or modern, put him to sleep.

The affair with my eye and my whistling in my first school occurred on the threshold of my teens, and they had long-lasting effects that contributed to the shaping of my whole life. The loss of the eye kept me out of the first World War, and I will tell as I go on what that meant to me. The whistling brought me out of the *Realschule* and started me on Latin and Greek instead of English and French. I adjusted well to life in this school. I was one of the best wrestlers in my class, thanks to continuous scuffles with my brother at home.

However, after several years I became restless. I began to feel that I would be learning more at a state gymnasium with its higher standards. Two other boys and I got together and decided to do the extra work that it would take to prepare ourselves to enter a better school. This was entirely my own choice. My parents, again, left the matter for me to decide. The other boys and I tried to make it clear to the authorities at the state school that it was our own decision to make this change. They appeared to be greatly perplexed; apparently they had never met with such a situation before. On the one hand, though surprising, it was a worthy and laudable ambition for boys to want to learn more, and they should be looked on with approval. On the other hand, the fact that our parents had only acquiesced but had not made the decision aroused their suspicions. It seemed to smack of insubordination, rebellion, or mutiny. Children should wait for their parents to tell them what to do; so we three changelings had to undergo a long cross-examination. It was a curious situation, and I was probably right in my feeling that the examiners were more embarrassed than the examinees. Anyway, the upshot was that we were accepted.

I was reminded of the way my father handled this situation and others when, much later, at a meeting, the anthropologist Gregory Bateson asked me about my upbringing in what he assumed must have been a strictly authoritarian society. I had to disappoint him when I described my father's attitude toward life and his children. But actually, I doubt whether the children of many Austrian families were given this much freedom to make decisions that were important for their lives.

In this new state gymnasium my best friend was the son of the commanding officer of the military forces that were stationed in Graz. He was the first person who talked to me about a coming war. One day—probably in 1912—we went for a walk in the woods, and he suggested that it would be a good idea for us to practice scouting. He said, "Let's run away from each other far enough so we can't see each other anymore. Then let each of us try to sneak up on the other. The one who comes closest without being caught will be the winner." I started playing the game, but I soon gave it up. I was apparently an incorrigible civilian and could not quite enter into this military exercise. It seemed to me ridiculous for sixteen-year-old boys to crawl around in the woods and play such a childish game. But when I protested, my friend became quite serious and said that there would certainly be a big war within the next few years and that all the young people would have to learn to scout and sneak up on hostile sentries and that we had better get ready by playing warlike games in advance.

During this time the pleasure in writing never left me, and I acquired the habit of always having a notebook into which I could record whatever came into my mind. I still have the notebooks from those days, and reading them brings back the prewar years as nothing else could. They are not systematic diaries but a mixture of notes about things that happened and trips that we took during vacations, of observations of myself and other people, and of fantastic little stories. Since this present account deals with the development of my ideas related to psychology as well as with events of my life, I may mention a theory about happiness that I first thought of when I was maybe thirteen or fourteen years old. This theory implied that happiness and unhappiness in a person's life are sooner or later balanced or equalized. One is somehow recompensed for unhappiness, and one will always have to pay for happy times. I also applied that idea to expectations: if one is very happy in looking forward to an event, he will certainly be disappointed; it won't measure up to the expectation. On the other hand, if one greatly dreads something and suffers ahead of time, what actually occurs will not at all be so bad. Maybe there was a dim recognition in this theory that an expectation sets a level. If one expects too much and sets the level too high, then almost any actual experience will be a disappointment, and the joy of expectation will be followed by some degree of sadness. The opposite will happen when the level is set too low.

When I was fifteen, I wrote a little story about a boy who could choose what the first half of his life would be like. Of course, he chose a life of great happiness, one in which he would be rich and fortunate. Then, in middle age, he suddenly lost everything. He tried to kill himself, but fate would not let him go, and he had to pay for his early happiness by living in a mental institution for the second half of his life. This theory of a happiness balance seems to me a very obvious one, something that quite a few people have probably formulated in more convincing ways. As far as I can remember, I did not get the idea from anything I read or heard. But it seems to have served a good purpose for my personal life. My early emotional responses to the good and bad strokes of fortune had been rather excessive, and this theory somewhat dampened them and evened them out.

During my teens there was a significant change in my personality, probably typical to some degree of adolescence. As a small child, I was said to have been a highly extroverted chatterbox, talking and laughing all the time. Then, when I was about fourteen, I became a very silent person, introverted, and exceedingly shy. It may have been partly the

9

result of the eye injury, though this actually showed itself only three or four years after the accident. Still, even at this time when I had become very shy, I kept on reaching out and trying to find others with whom I could really talk, people interested in "higher" things. This period during adolescence, when I was silent and serious, was very important for my development. It was then that I acquired the habit of introspection, though certainly the beginnings had arisen much earlier. Anyway, at that time I was always watching and evaluating my thoughts, feelings, and attitudes, all the fascinating objects of the inner world.

During these years my family and the families of some of our relatives spent part of their summers in a big house that one of our ancestors had built a few miles out of Graz, in a village known as Feistritz. Perhaps I should interrupt my narrative to tell a little about the extended family, many of whose members will come into my story. My father's father, also named Moriz, whom I never knew, was one of the first scientific dentists of Austria and became dentist to the imperial family. He was a man of strong democratic principles, and when the Emperor Franz Joseph wanted him to accept a title, perhaps with the thought that dental care was still more painful when it was administered by a commoner, a mere Dr. Heider, he refused the honor. When he invented a tooth powder, he did not patent it: if it were of use, it should be for all the people without extra charge.

This dentist had four children. One son, Adolf, became a physician. He died while he was still young, probably from typhoid fever contracted in his efforts, as an early ecologist, to rid the Danube of pollution. Then there was Karl, a professor of zoology. He had a daughter, Doris, to whom I became close as I was growing up. My father, the youngest of the sons, who became an architect in Graz, had much of the Styrian outlook. He liked to dress in the costume of gray and green wool that many Grazers wore, and he often fell

The house at Feistritz

into the dialect of the region. He was somewhat scornful of academic life and what he saw as the pompousness of many professors.

There was also a daughter, Jetti, in the dentist's family, who was married to a professor of economics in Vienna. They had five children, Stephan and Lilly, who were enough older that we were never companions as children, and Max, Alex, and Hilda, who were more the ages of my brother and myself. This family belonged very much to the Viennese setting, and the boys had learned the social graces like "kissing the hand" and making a formal bow, as my brother and I were never expected to do. I especially remember my youthful scorn of the ladylike ways of Lilly, the elder daughter. Many years later the American wife of Stephan remarked to my American wife, "Of course, they (meaning

11

my brother and myself) were terribly spoiled." But the Feistritz house, where all of us met at different times, did a great deal to create a feeling of the family as a unit in spite of many differences. I may add that a few years later, during the First World War, Lilly stayed in Feistritz with her children while her husband was in the army. I saw a good deal of her then and came genuinely to like her and to enjoy being with her.

As I think back on the Feistritz house, I recall an anecdote of my parents' early married life. My father was teaching my mother to ride a bicycle. They decided to practice in the privacy of the spacious attic, where there were a few loose boards that seem to have given off a rumbling noise that sounded like thunder to people on the floor below as the bicycle was ridden back and forth. Two of my father's elderly aunts, who had scientific interests, were living in the house. They mailed regular accounts of the Feistritz weather to the Graz newspaper—this being before the day of regular weather reporting and easy telephone communication, amateur reports like these were welcomed. According to the press, the weather that summer presented some unusual features: the skies were consistently clear and blue, yet daily periods of thunder were reported from the Feistritz area.

My mother's father, Eugen von Halaczy, originally Hungarian, was a Viennese physician who spent the summer months with his family in Mauer, near Vienna, where I often visited when I was a little boy. By that time my grandfather had given up his regular practice to become medical examiner for an insurance company. The hours of this position gave him freedom to spend time on his special hobby of botany. He wrote a book, in Latin, on the plants of Greece, and he collected plants for his garden. A few years ago when we had lunch with Walter and Lore Toman, who spend part of their year in Mauer, I was happy to find the house where my grandparents had lived there and to see some of my grandfather's plants still flourishing in the garden.

I may add here that botany was another of my father's hobbies and that it was through this interest that he had come to know my grandfather and to meet my mother. My grandfather was well known among the botanists of Vienna, and the two men became better acquainted when another botanist took my father to one of the informal meetings that were held at my grandfather's home. When my grandfather was writing his book on the plants of Greece, my father accompanied him on one of his trips to that region.

Later, after my father had moved to Graz, he became interested in diatoms, a form of microscopic algae that look like crystal jewels. He wrote a book on the diatoms of Styria, which he illustrated with many beautiful pen-and-ink drawings. I know that he gave the manuscript to the botanical museum in Graz, but I do not know whether it was ever published.

To go back to my boyhood, I remember when my cousin Alex and I started reading about the philosophy of India. This interest may have begun partly because my father, as a young man studying architecture, had traveled to India and brought back watercolor paintings that he made there. Alex and I felt that one way to get acquainted with what interested us about India would be to learn the language of the holy scriptures, so we ordered Sanskrit dictionaries and learned the alphabet. We also read collections of stories and translated one story from Sanskrit into German. And for maybe two years, when we were apart, we wrote to each other using the Sanskrit alphabet.

All through those years my father was the comrade whom I admired and with whom I could discuss many of my personal and theoretical problems. He was a no-nonsense person who made fun of me when I got lost in abstract speculations. When I think of him, I remember a saying that he was fond of using when he wanted to convince me of the futility of one of my ideas. He would say, "You can't get a dog out from behind a stove with that argument." He was thinking of the way a dog sticks to a warm spot in winter.

Other memories from that time are of our summer vacations. The early ones were trips by train, when the four of us traveled together. Later my mother began to find these rail trips tiring. My parents talked of buying a car and even had one on approval for a few days. My father began to take driving lessons, but my mother distrusted this new means of locomotion. In the end, my father bought a motorcycle with a sidecar, in which my brother and I rode, and the three of us explored Styria with it during the next years. Its motor was not powerful enough to take three passengers up the hills of the region, and we boys often leaped out and helped push it when it threatened to stall, then managed to clamber back on as my father began to steer it slowly downhill. Every so often we came to an out-of-the-way village where people who had never seen such a vehicle before stared as we passed through, making it still more of an adventure for us.

It was during the years at the gymnasium, maybe around 1913, that the word *Gestalt* came especially to my attention. It was used by my father in the sense of a regular geometrical form. As I have told, my father had a number of hobbies, including painting and drawing, with which he busied himself outside of the hours when he worked as an architect. He was especially interested in visual experience, and he thought a lot about it. Like all German-speaking people of his day, he was familiar with Goethe's ideas, some of which came close to what was later to be known as gestalt psychology. I have a sheet of paper on which he drew figures made up of dots and straight lines that seem almost to have come from one of Max Wertheimer's later papers on unit formation. The notes he made on that page include the statement that I translate as "the parts of a lawful gestalt

14

have such relations to each other that they cannot be arbitrarily substituted by other parts." I may mention that the word he actually employed was *Gestalt*, since it was fairly common in German before it was often used in English. My father considered his ideas about simple forms important. He never published about them, but once he gave a talk on problems related to them to a club of architects and invited me to hear him explain them. Later, when I heard more about the gestalt idea at the university in lectures on the psychology of perception, I had the feeling of having an especially intimate relation with it through my father—a sort of affectionate kinship.

One more aspect of my gymnasium years I mention here because of the way it continued into what I think of as a different stage of my life. Like many adolescents, I was haunted by questions about the meaning of life: What makes life worthwhile? What kind of life should I choose? The reason for my decision to exchange the lazy life at the private school for that of the more demanding state school was that I asked myself these questions. It gave me pleasure to formulate problems in which values such as happiness and goodness were opposed to their opposites. For instance, would it be more desirable for people to be happy and foolish or to be unhappy and wise? Which would you prefer for yourself? What would you rather be—a mediocre but popular painter or a good one whose work was not recognized? These are the kinds of puzzles I brooded about until I found myself in a sort of exaggerated puritanism. I despised everything that smacked of the social amenities, I hated empty chitchat, I thought that drinking and smoking were abominable, and I had a feeling of superiority on the days when my mother spent an afternoon playing cards and drinking coffee with a few friends. I tried to exclude any sort of frivolity from my life.

I worked hard at my school subjects, tried to learn several languages by myself, and read only serious books. At the same time, the transitoriness and vanity of human life often came to me, though it was usually only part of a passing mood. I remember just one time when it suddenly seemed real—I even remember where I was sitting when the conviction of the futility of human life overwhelmed me with the power of a great storm or tidal wave. I realized that though I had toyed with the idea before, I had never taken it seriously. I was struck by the thought of our small planet rolling through the universe, of the way man had appeared on it, struggled and labored, and by the thought that it would all collapse and disappear. For the most part these thoughts did not make me unhappy; instead, they made me feel free and at ease. Life had been a heavy burden to me, and the thought that things were not necessarily so serious and important was not altogether unpleasant. The full realization of this idea lasted only a short time, one particular afternoon, but its shadow stayed with me in a half-unreal shape for a long time. It is likely that many adolescents go through similar experiences, especially now in the day of the atom bomb.

If I think back on my life as it developed during the years at the gymnasium, I cannot help feeling that the direction in which my interests eventually settled was fully prepared during that time. There already existed the concern with problems of perception, the interest in sketching, which means attempts to fashion convincing two-dimensional representations of three-dimensional reality. There was also the continuing preoccupation with ideas about people and their interactions, which was to become intensified during the hard years of the war. This included a growing attempt to theorize and to try to solve agonizing personal problems by working toward a clear conceptual understanding of them. Close to this was an early interest in geography. I loved maps. Whenever I was in bed with one of the diseases that beset children, I was given the big family atlas and was happy poring over the maps that reminded me of the trips we had taken. I could easily see myself as a future geographer.

But there was another angle to this interest. It always, then and later, gave me great pleasure to make a survey of whatever region I was in and to understand how its parts were related. Maybe this gave me a feeling of control over the environment. When I was about fifteen, I asked my father to give me a surveyor's kit, and I made a sort of map of the country near Graz. Whenever I was in a strange city, I bought a map of the city and its surroundings first thing. With this map I would then climb to the highest point around, often a church tower, and try to get a good idea of the topography of the region. As I look back, I believe that this desire to clarify the geographical setting showed later in my need to make theories. I am never satisfied with a specific limited area in my thinking; I always want to understand the relations between concepts and ideas. And when I read experimental papers, I want to place their results and find out how they fit in with what I think of as the map of psychology. I am uncomfortable when I cannot relate them to other landmarks.

There was one peculiarity in the composition of my abilities that appeared already during my school days and often puzzled me. We were regularly required to write little "essays" as home work, and I found these assignments especially difficult. I would get all tense, and my brain seemed to refuse to work. I usually got poor marks on the papers I finally completed. On the other hand, it was easy to write the observations and stories that went into my notebooks. It was as though I was writing when I was "full of it," and the material more or less wrote itself. It was the literary tasks imposed from outside that were difficult for me. And all the time I saw other boys who were excellent at assigned writing but who were unable to do anything on their own.

WORLD WAR I: UNIVERSITY YEARS
AND MY FIRST JOB

At the beginning of the summer of 1914, when I was eighteen, I passed the final examination of the gymnasium and had to decide what to do next. At that stage of my life I was a very introverted and unhappy person, ignorant of the ways of the world and leading the life of a hermit. By this time the idea of becoming a geographer had faded, though the interest in geography has remained with me. I played with the idea of becoming a writer, but during the last half of my gymnasium years I had gradually decided that I wanted to be a painter. I always had an easel standing in my room, often with a half-finished painting displayed on it; and when we went on a trip, I usually took a sketchbook with me. In general, visual meaning and expression remained an important part of experience for me. But my father discouraged the idea of either writing or painting as a career. He said that one should not treat the muses as cows to be milked to provide one's sustenance. Instead, they are women to be loved, and the arts they represent should be revered. He talked about his own life as an architect who spent his mornings in his office or at the site of a half-finished building he had designed and had the rest of his time for his hobbies. He suggested, ''Why don't you study architecture? That fits in well with a hobby of painting.'' I followed this advice and enrolled in the Technical School in Graz, after spending two months in intensive study to prepare for an entrance examination in calculus.

In the meantime, World War I had begun in August. I tried to enlist right away but was rejected because of the injury to my eye. I became still more lonely than before, as I felt that I was missing out on the experience that other members of my generation were having. My brother, my cousins, and most of my school friends were in the service, whereas I got only as far as the Home Guard, carrying a gun as I walked the streets at night or guarded munitions stored at the railroad station. One memory from this time seems to have been deeply imprinted: whenever I hear the distant sound of dogs barking in the darkness, I am reminded of those nights when I was on guard in a little village on the outskirts of Graz.

I was altogether miserable. Also, I began to feel that architecture was not the right thing for me. I had spent a good deal of the first semester making meticulous drawings of classical columns and was utterly bored. I explained my feelings to my father, and he suggested that I study law. As a lawyer I could find jobs that would leave me time for hobbies, he said.

I could not enter law school until autumn, and during the interval I worked on a project that my father had thought about and made starts on for several years. Like many of that period, he was fascinated by the possibility of flying, by balloon, by glider, or by airplane. He had studied Leonardo da Vinci's writings and drawings on the subject and had considered the possibility of building a glider in which a man could rise into the air and fly as the birds seemed to do so easily. I shared his enthusiasm and set out for Feistritz to see what I could do with a supply of bamboo that he had collected. I hoped at least to make a machine that would produce movement along the ground as a driver supplied the energy to make it flap its wings, but the material proved to be too heavy. I think of that attempt when I occasionally see on TV a man-powered glider made of the featherweight synthetics that are produced by modern technology.

This took up much of my time between my semester of architecture and the fall of 1915, when I enrolled in law school. However, I soon found law as dull as architecture had been. Austrian legal education of that day began with a heavy dose of memorizing Roman law, and I was never good at memorizing. I told my father that I would like just to go to the university without any definite study plan. There were so many interesting courses that I would like to attend as an auditor. I didn't want to take examinations, which in any case were given only at the end of a program, not after single courses. My father agreed, but he reminded me that eventually I would have to support myself, for the family was not wealthy, and I could not get on without a job. In the end he suggested that I attend the university on my own for four years, then study some kind of agriculture. I might raise pigs on the family land near the Feistritz house. Pigs were nice animals, he said. I agreed, of course; I was nineteen years old, and four years seemed a very long time. Something more interesting than pigs might turn up when those four years were over.

Anyway, I was happy to follow this plan, attending a variety of lectures at the university from premedical courses to philosophy and art history. Also, after the custom in Germany and Austria, I spent time at other universities. In the summer semester of 1917 I went to Innsbruck to study zoology with Uncle Karl, who was teaching there at that time. In the spring of 1918 I was in Munich studying psychology with Karl and Charlotte Bühler. Karl gave a course in child psychology, and Charlotte gave a laboratory course in experimental psychology. These were the first lectures I attended that treated psychological subjects systematically. I met the assistant at the Munich Psychological Institute, Kurt Huber, a very attractive and interesting person who was writing a thesis on the psychology of music. I had many discussions with him and got to like him very much. In later years he became an active anti-Nazi. He worked with two students, a brother and sister, the "Geschwister Scholl," distributing pamphlets against the Hitler government. In 1943 all three were caught and executed.

When I returned to Graz, I soon gave up the extensive sampling of courses in different fields and began to concentrate on philosophy and, as far as that was possible, on psychology. Alexius Meinong was certainly the teacher who had the greatest influence on my thinking. He had a commanding presence, in spite of his short stature, and always gave the impression of being a well-organized person with extraordinary intelligence. He was almost blind, something that he tried to hide as far as possible. His lectures dealt only tangentially with psychological problems. Those that I attended treated theories of probability, of value, and epistemology. In his seminars we usually read a book together and discussed it. The central feature of Meinong's philosophy and psychology was the idea that he took from his teacher, Franz Brentano, which in contemporary terms might be designated as "intentionality" or "symbolic representation." I do not know whether this idea was already familiar to me before I attended Meinong's lectures, though as I look back, it seems to me that I have always had the conviction that thought and perceptions are "about" something in a way that the fall of a stone is not "about" anything. I seem to have more or less forgotten not only his firm distinctions between content and object of ideas but also the rest of his treatment of intention. I don't think I ever had a real feeling for their importance. The fact that I attended Meinong's lectures and seminars year after year does not mean that I was greatly impressed by what he had to say. I had very much the feeling about Meinong that Brentano had: Brentano was especially critical of Meinong's claim that he was discovering more and more mental objects. Brentano saw this as a revival of some of the bad features of scholasticism, a sort of fanciful and capricious hairsplitting.

If I try to go back to the impression that I had of Meinong's philosophy at the time, I would say that it seemed cold and lifeless, a chilly marble temple constructed by a man with a complicated brain but no heart. But now, after all these years, I find that I have a more positive feeling about Meinong and his lectures and books. There is certainly one side of his abstract speculations that leaves me cold, probably because I don't fully understand it. But I must add that it was just this aspect of his thought that was so stimulating to the British philosophers like Bertrand Russell and G. E. Moore, both of whom wrote long papers on Meinong. For example, there is the problem of the existence of impossible objects. Some people think that in raising such questions, Meinong was touching on something that is very basic to our mental lives. But I have the suspicion that these problems arise out of an abuse of language, or perhaps out of a misunderstanding of language.

Beside this aspect of Meinong's thinking, there is another that comes out when he deals with the more concrete questions of *probability* and *value*, and with his more detailed discussions of the commonsense versions of these ideas. I must have learned a lot from his reflections on these problems, and I find that I can still read some passages of his work with profit.

Another important figure in the Graz Institute was the Italian Vittorio Benussi, a former student of Meinong's. He was an elegant-looking, lean person with a finely chiseled and melancholy face and a dry, skeptical smile. He went around in a black laboratory smock, and when he took a walk, he wore a black hat with a wide brim and puffed on a long black cigar. One year there was a student who often walked with him, much shorter but in exactly the same outfit. Benussi mostly worked in a darkened room, where he had a cot along with his apparatus, and he often spent the night as well as the day there. He did not give many courses, perhaps because his health was not good. I remember one course in which he used the students as subjects for a whole semester in an experiment on guessing the number of dots in a long series of patterns. He did this without giving us any idea of the purpose of the experiment. I finally rebelled and told him humbly that I would like to learn psychology from him. He was very friendly, gave me a key to the laboratory,

Vittorio Benussi

and said that all the apparatus was at my disposal but that he did not have much time.

Benussi came from Trieste, which at that time belonged to Austria, and he spoke with an Italian accent. His father had strong Italian and anti-Austrian sentiments, and the young Benussi must have shared them and all the time must have felt himself an outsider in Graz. At the end of World War I he became an Italian citizen, finally becoming professor at Padua, where I saw him in 1926. I had a feeling then that he was rather depressed and homesick for Graz. He had made a respected place for himself in Austrian and German psychology and may not immediately have received the same recognition among Italian psychologists, though today he is certainly an important figure for them. He died when he was not quite fifty years old, a marginal man who stood between two cultures. He was one of the first to make experiments in the field of gestalt perception, and when Wertheimer's famous paper appeared in 1912, Benussi had already published a long series of studies. The Berlin group had great respect for him, using some of his demonstrations in their treatment of gestalt principles, though their theoretical approaches were somewhat different.

I should also say a few words about Hugo Spitzer, who was another professor at the University of Graz at that time. He and my Uncle Karl were old friends. He had an encyclopedic mind and was at home equally in all the bypaths of the history of philosophy and the newest publications concerning psychology or the natural sciences. I remember taking a course from him on the pre-Socratic philosophers and one on brain lesions. His suits were usually incredibly dirty, and we had the feeling that we could have told what he had eaten for breakfast on any particular day from the multicolored spots on the front of his vest. However, his hands were always meticulously clean and delicate and white like a lady's.

I always remember one incident that occurred after I had taken my degree. I had been away, and when I returned to Graz, I went to see Spitzer. While I was talking with him, a second visitor came, another professor at the university. Right away the two of them began a lively discussion of administration policy, which they did in a curious language consisting mainly of Latin expressions and all sorts of old-fashioned formalisms. I was quite put off and thought, "So this is how they talk to each other!" They seemed to me to be two antediluvians, completely out of touch with present-day reality. Listening to their ceremonious elaborations made me think again of my father's criticisms of university life. However, not many years later, I experienced a complete reorganization of the meaning of the episode, a reorganization in Wertheimer's sense. I realized that the two professors had used this stilted, old-fashioned way of speaking, not because that was the way they usually talked to each other, but because they did not want me to understand what they were talking about, doubtless some official faculty business.

Among the students I met at Meinong's lectures and seminars was one who became a close friend, Otto

Hartmann. Through him I met others who became important to me, and I, in turn, influenced his life as we kept in close touch through the rest of my years in Europe. I saw him last when I was in Graz in 1970, but when I tried to see him again in 1976, I heard that he had left for some unknown place, so I do not know whether he is still living. He was a highly gifted person. While he was still in the gymnasium, he had published about twenty papers on plant physiology in scientific journals. When I first got to know him, he had left plant physiology and was spending all his time on philosophy. We soon arranged to get together regularly for discussions. These meetings were a great pleasure to me, and when I walked home from one of them, I had a feeling that I had soared to great heights and that I had to unwind gradually and come down to earth again. Otto was a formidable thinker, and though he had come to philosophy from very down-to-earth experiments in a natural science, he was already leaning toward mystical and grandiose generalizations. But because he had a broad knowledge of modern science and of the history of philosophy, his ideas were fascinating and always provided a starting point for fruitful discussions. Usually I played the role of the sober-minded realist who brought Otto back to common sense with a joke when he had gone too far in flights of romantic philosophy. In later years his outlook was very much influenced by Rudolf Steiner, the founder of anthroposophy. Otto wrote a good many books from this point of view, dealing with a wide range of topics in philosophy, biology, medicine, literature, and science. I have read a few of them and found a wealth of insights in them. Although I cannot accept all of his theories, I do not understand why they are not more widely known.

Another person who became very significant in my life at that time was Uncle Karl's daughter, Doris, who was four years older than I. We had not seen much of each other when we were children, but during the war years her family and mine, along with the family from Vienna, were together more often in the Feistritz house. In a short time, Doris and I became very good friends. I called her my sister, though I was more or less in love with her. She scolded me for this, and I am sure that neither of us would have let this relationship go beyond friendship. Doris herself had earlier gone through a long undiagnosed illness from which she had since recovered. This experience had made her mature and thoughtful, and in her life in the sanitorium, where she spent part of her teens, she had come to know a variety of people very well. She had a lot of common sense, was cheerful and friendly, and was just the person to help me break away from the depressed state into which I had fallen and to help me deal with my immature convictions and my exaggerated self-consciousness. She told me that I was too much occupied with myself and that my ideas about other people were mostly cockeyed. But even when she argued against the excesses into which the observations of myself and other people had brought me, she recognized that, in many cases, my analyses of specific actions were correct.

During the next years, Doris and I exchanged voluminous letters when we were apart, and we were often together in the summers. Now that I have mentioned those letters, one of her observations that startled me and gave me to think comes to my mind. I often wrote her about my extensive daydreams and how they entertained me, especially when I was taking long solitary walks across the countryside. She had always viewed my tendency to reverie and daydreaming as evidence of my odd and maybe unhealthy peculiarities. But to my surprise, there came a letter in which she told me that she had suddenly realized that she also had daydreams and that she had had them frequently and for a long time. I was greatly startled—how was it possible that this sort of fantasy had been part of her life for a long time without her being aware of it and that she now suddenly realized it? I will not try to solve the problem that this raises, but certainly it seems to show that self-awareness or self-observation is more complicated than one would suspect.

Attending the university lectures and seminars, as well as the companionship of Doris and Otto and other students whom I came to know through Otto, greatly changed the color of my life, though my genuine interest in psychological observation and philosophical speculation continued. I should add that this was not simply a matter of cold, scientific curiosity. Frequently It was aroused by deeply felt experiences and painful conflicts of value that I tried to understand and control by looking hard at them and analyzing them.

Perhaps these ideas were especially strong with me because they helped me to deal with my shyness. In spite of the facts that I had given up my hermit life and that I had Doris and Otto as friends, I still often felt that the pressure of other people was overpowering. I tried to describe this peculiar influence exerted by people to myself: when one enters a room, one gets a general impression of it, of its size, of the brightness of the illumination, of the color of its walls, and of the kind of furniture. But all this is usually outweighed by reactions to the presence or absence of other persons in the room; and if other people are present, it makes a great difference in our reactions whether they are familiar persons or strangers, whether they are people we like or not, and, in general, what our relation to them is.

What is it that makes persons so unique in their influence on our feelings about the environment? I tried out different possibilities in my imagination. For instance, would the pressure of people be so salient if we were to think of them as being merely complicated machines? It was thoughts of this kind that formed the background of a short story that I wrote at about that time (1919). I will sketch the content of the story that I called ''The Concert'': A scholar leaves his study and walks down the street. He is hypersensitive, and the behavior of the people whom he sees disturbs him. He feels that they all act like animals or like automata, like puppets that are guided by wires. He sees an announcement of a concert and decides to attend it. As he sits in the concert hall, he asks himself: "Is this feeling that people are puppets just a pale, abstract thought? Is this thought real for me?" He decides to test himself by doing something that he could only do if he were truly convinced that he was surrounded by puppets, something he would never do if he believed that human beings were around. He decides to stand up in the midst of the concert, to go to the conductor's podium, and to pull at his trousers so as to make him fall. Our hero fails the test miserably and in a ridiculous way. First of all, he does not quite reach the conductor's trouser leg. The audience gets angry at the interruption that he has created. Suddenly, human feelings arise and completely defeat the morbid thoughts that have been analyzing, dissecting, and killing all his natural emotions. Ancient godlike forms appear before him, and he watches them as they come, one after another—Pity, Anger, Joy, Love, and Fellowship. He breaks down and is taken out of the room.

In this story I was attempting to describe some of the dangers of psychological analysis. It can lead to a certain presumption and arrogance when others are seen as mere puppets without freedom and human dignity. The psychologist who stands outside to observe and explain their mechanisms may feel himself the only exception, the only real person. This is an unnatural attitude that is in conflict with deep-seated beliefs about people, and in the end these convictions overcome the abstract constructions. In a way it is a victory for common sense.

Another example of my thoughts about people as automata is what I called "the existential walk." It suddenly came to me one day that I myself rarely acted as a free agent, that most of the time I was bound by previous decisions. When I went for a walk, I usually decided before I started where I would go and about how long I would stay out.

Then, unless some unexpected event interfered, the actual walk would roll off automatically. I asked myself, "Is it really true that I often act like an automaton?" I had always hated the idea of people acting like machines, like puppets. So I decided, for once, not to decide in advance. I just started out, not knowing where I would go or how far—I would decide every minute or so what I would do the next minute. In my wanderings, I came to the railroad station, bought a ticket without feeling any obligation to use it up, and only decided at each station whether to ride further or get off the train. I passed maybe three stations, then I left the train and roamed about in a minute-by-minute fashion. But what I found was that these endless decisions were so exhausting that after another hour I made the decision to go straight home again.

This whole exercise had been very strenuous, and when I got home, I felt as worn out as if I had climbed a high mountain. I lay down on the nearest sofa. Years later I thought back to this walk when I heard Sartre tell about his prison experience. He said that it was not so bad—it was comfortable not to have to make decisions.

There was another time when I tried to get what would now be called a "sensory deprivation" experience. There is a mountain with many caves near Feistritz. I went far enough into one of these caves so that no light could be seen from outside. I lay down on a mattress that I had brought along, put out the candle by whose light I had found my way, stopped my watch, then waited, to see how long I could stand it to lie there in complete isolation and darkness. Unfortunately, I soon found that I was not at all deprived of sensory experience. There were sensations from the hard little mattress and also from a steady drip of water that was trickling through the limestone rocks. What I enjoyed most after perhaps an hour were images like abstract moving pictures that began to appear in color. And I had underestimated the coldness of the rocky ground. After a while the cold began to permeate the mattress, and I felt that my bones would soon freeze. I crawled to the opening of the cave after I had been in it for over twelve hours. I looked out over the valley below me and at the mountains on the other side, with the evening sun just disappearing behind them. I will never forget this picture because the colors were of a brilliance and a beauty that I had never seen before and have never seen since. I do not quite understand this effect. It could not have been simply that my eyes were rested from the long stay in the darkness of the cave. They rest every night without providing such a spectacle.

At this point I should say something about the situation in which I and my family were living. The war went on, and I tried several times more to enter the military service. I began to wonder whether I was rejected because the draft board considered the possibility that my injured eye might become infected and affect the healthy eye. So, on one bleak, wintry day in 1916 I went to the hospital, accompanied by my father, and had the damaged eye removed, to be replaced by an artificial one. But even after that change in my physical condition, I was not taken on.

As the months passed, more and more restrictions were placed on food, heat, and light, and I came to realize that my mother must be having a difficult time just feeding the family. As a little child I had loved her dearly and thought that she was a wonderful person with her musical gift and her gay, outgoing ways. But as I was growing into adolescence, I had felt closer to my father, while my mother and I had seemed to go our separate ways and to have fewer interests in common. This may have come about partly because she was not entirely well during those years; she seemed to suffer from strange ailments. I wonder now whether she had not developed allergies that made her heart pound and brought on periods of fretfulness and depression.

However, I remember with pleasure a time in 1918, during my university years, when I had just returned from Munich. I was with her for two weeks in Feistritz, and we had long, affectionate talks. She was her old, amusing self. She even played the piano again for me, and as I lay there on the sofa listening, I thought how little one needs in order to be happy. Hardly a month later she had died in the influenza epidemic of that year, which swept Europe as well as other parts of the world.

After this, my father and I moved to a house on the other side of the city. My brother was still in the army, but distant relatives were often with us and also Nora, the wife of my brother, and their small daughter, Ilse. Food was scarce, and in the evening we all sat around a single oil lamp that gave just enough light for us to read and write. A general atmosphere of animosity and resentment developed, and every so often, one of us would lose his temper at something that another happened to do. I hated the mutual accusations and bickering, and I tried to stay out of it. It is natural that I fell back on my old standby, namely to observe what was going on, recording and trying to analyze the troubles. I think I must have felt that by examining the course of anger in others, I would be able to master and digest my own anger, that perhaps I could transform my resentments into something innocuous and thus dissolve their power to make me unhappy. I do not know where I acquired the strong conviction that outbreaks of temper are usually demeaning and silly; probably from my parents in happier times.

I did not try to make experiments, but I began collecting and writing down observations of typical cases in which connections between origins and consequences seemed to be particularly obvious. I often exaggerated what came to seem typical of these anger situations and in this way obtained a kind of caricature. Thus, in thinking about them, I was trying to find general concepts and general causal connections. To phrase it in terms that I learned a few years later from Kurt Lewin, I was trying to get hold of genotypical, underlying concepts, not just surface manifestations. Because of this orientation in my thinking, I did not go about making observations in a Baconian way of simply collecting one example after another and computing averages. Of course, what I was doing at that stage was merely a matter of intuitive groping—I was not working according to a consciously formulated method. Only now, when I go back to my notes on these first attempts to study a psychological problem, I realize that I was soon using approaches that were congenial to Lewin's thinking. And what luck it was that I came to know him during my Berlin years and was able to learn from him.

I still have quite a few of these notes on anger, which I have never tried to organize or summarize. These are observations either on the background state of irritation when one seeks a legitimate reason for a full-blown outbreak or on the relation between the anger and the cause to which we attribute it. Anger toward a person means: "It is *his* fault. He ought to be reproved or punished." If we come to feel that he is not to blame, the anger that is directed against him loses its meaning. Other notes deal with playing the martyr, with the effects of suppressed anger, with the relation of anger to feelings of right and wrong. There are no references to academic psychological literature, but there are quotations from Nietzsche, Schopenhauer, La Rochefoucauld, and Ibsen.

I also wrote a number of short sketches to illustrate the role of anger in one's personal life and social relationships. One of these sketches deals with two women who had not had enough to eat for months—a reflection of my experience of the war days. A pot of soup is on their table. They are strongly drawn to it, but because they are well brought up and genteel, they pretend to ignore it. They prolong the preliminaries before they begin to eat; neither wants to show how hungry she is. This suppression makes for a groundswell of anger that is built up in each of them. There is a kind of contest to see who can wait longer. For either to show the suppressed frustration and irritation that comes from her long-endured hunger would represent a defeat. A kind of game follows, in which each tries to make the other one show her greed. Finally the soup is served into the two bowls that stand beside the pot. One of the women brings her dish toward her with a jerk that spills some of the precious soup. She can no longer contain her irritation. She loses her temper and makes a spiteful remark. The other pretends to be very concerned with the accident; she helps to wipe up the spilled soup while she gloats over her victory.

These outbreaks of anger and my efforts to make sense of them finally led me to the conclusion that the source of trouble lies in the egotism and egocentricity of people; in making this generalization, I definitely included myself. Each person is convinced that he has certain rights, and if another violates these rights, then he will defend them like a dog whose territory has been invaded by the mailman. I remember dimly that this pervading power of egotism disturbed me at first, especially because I realized that I was just like everyone else in this respect. However, I recovered more or less, maybe with the help of a trifling sophistry: I decided that a certain degree of egotism is necessary for life and is not really unhealthy; and I cheerfully accepted the fact that I was also ''sinful.'' For a while I talked with my father about my observations regarding anger and my theories about them, but I gradually gave it up, because he felt that these thoughts were morbid, and I could see that it troubled him to discuss them.

I have a feeling that in this study of anger, many of my later ideas about interpersonal events and person perception were already being applied, though certainly in an embryonic form, and that it was a big step in building the background of what I would eventually come to. And though I do not want to spell this out in detail, I will add a few remarks about egocentric perception. It often happened that after a quarrel in which I was not involved, I would talk with both of the antagonists and would obtain a different description of what had happened from each of them. For each one, his version was true and objective, and it was what he had perceived with his own eyes and ears. In terms used by psychologists who study the perceptions of formal manifolds, the data are organized in different ways by the two participants. Parenthetically, I may mention that most of these psychologists have used two-dimensional geometrical patterns drawn on paper or projected on a screen rather than interpersonal situations. Anyway, in my studies about anger, I often had occasion to observe this influence of subjective factors on perception and cognition and the ways in which each person interpreted what was given in the stimuli so that it harmonized with his own preconceptions and thereby showed that he was noble and that his antagonist, at best, was full of egocentric delusions.

Besides these pursuits that contain the germs of my later psychology of personal relations, I also continued to occupy myself with speculations concerning general perception and cognition of objects. As I have said, I always felt that this interest had its roots in my pleasure in drawing and sketching. About 1917 I made what I thought at the time was an interesting discovery, one that helped me break through the unhappiness of that period. It made me believe in myself, and it strengthened me. It was a complex of thoughts having to do with structures of events and well-formed units. These thoughts eventually led me to the ideas that I treated in my doctoral thesis, which I will discuss later in this account. Here I will only mention briefly two short papers that I wrote at that time but never published.

One of these deals with the physiological processes that are responsible for the experience of unitary figures, or gestalts. It is the problem that Wolfgang Köhler later treated in detail in his 1920 book *Die physische Gestalten in Ruhe und im stationären Zustand* (which can be translated briefly as "Physical *Gestalten*"), with somewhat different conclusions. I agreed with Köhler only in that I too said that the underlying physiological processes must in some way be unitary, but I felt that their *effect* must also be unitary and characteristic for them. Soap bubbles, which are among

Köhler's examples, are unitary in that the events of the parts depend on certain properties of the whole, but the bubbles do not affect the environment in a unitary way that is specific to their form or state. They do not interact with other soap bubbles in ways that are characteristic of their forms. For instance, two soap bubbles do not form an action unit on the basis of their similarities, and so on.

Another of these short papers deals with relations between order and regularity, on the one hand, and the difference threshold on the other. It is maintained that slight changes will be noticed more easily with regular than with irregular forms. For example, let us consider distributions of twelve dots. When they are aligned in a straight row, they make a simple, regular figure, and if one of them is even a little out of place, it is very noticeable. On the other hand, if they are scattered in an irregular fashion, a change in the position of a single dot is not so easily spotted. I am sure that this has been demonstrated in experiments since my thoughts about it in 1917, but I do not happen to have run across reports of such experiments.

As I have told, I began attending lectures at the university in Graz and at other universities without planning to work for a degree. However, by the summer of 1919, my contemporaries, one after another, began to work on their dissertations, and I decided that I might as well try to do so. I went to Meinong, who had always been very nice to me, and told him that I would like to work on something related to perception. He referred me to one of his books with the title *Ueber die Erfahrungsgrundlagen unseres Wissens* (About the empirical basis of our knowledge). I bought the book right away and set myself to read it in my own room at home. I worked through the winter on the problems that Meinong touched upon. The winter was cold, but fortunately there was a piece of forest land belonging to the house where we lived at that time. I spent every morning in my unheated room, well covered with thick coats and gloves, writing what was to be my dissertation. Then I would go out with an ax, cut a little tree down, drag it home, and put it in the downstairs stove to warm the house a little. In my thesis I tried to solve the puzzles that Meinong posed in his book, among them one that deals with a simple causal theory of perception. This theory contends that we can see an object because it causes the processes that affect our eyes. In arguing against this theory, Meinong asked the following question: ''When I look at a house on which the sun is shining why do I say, 'I see the house'? Why do I not say, 'I see the sun'? It is, after all, the rays of the sun that cause the process.''

Thinking about this question led me to consider broader questions of causal structure and of transmission of information. The stimulus that reaches my eye does not change with a change in the form of the source of light, but it changes when there is a change in the illuminated object. When we look at a house in the sunlight, the information we receive is not about the shape of the sun but about the shape of the house. Whether the sun is round or square does not affect the proximal stimulus that reaches our eyes, but it matters for this stimulus whether the windows of the house are round or square. Therefore it is sensible to say that we see the house, not the sun.

A guiding thought of the thesis concerns the difference between things (including persons as environmental objects) and the mediation that transmits the information about things to our sense organs. It is easy to observe this difference for visual perception, but it is also involved in other senses. Solid objects are made up of parts that are dependent on each other to a large extent: if I pull on one part of a chair, the other parts will follow. The mediation, on the other hand, consists of parts of events that are mainly independent of each other. Insofar as the parts of a medium are tied together and are dependent on each other, the medium loses some of the possibility of transmitting messages. The difference between things and mediums is very important for perception, though in itself it is entirely a matter of the physical environment. It is independent of the sensory apparatus.

Thus the attempt to solve Meinong's puzzle started me on the consideration of the conditions of perception in the wider environment. It led me to distinguish the "proximal" from the "distal" stimulus and in this way eventually called attention to the great significance of causal attributions in our attempt to understand our environment. As a matter of fact, it was only recently, as I was immersing myself in the thoughts and atmosphere of what I was doing sixty years ago, that I realized how important Meinong's question has been for my thinking over the years.

I would like to mention that some twenty years later Bertrand Russell dealt with similar problems in his book *Human Knowledge*. Russell also starts with the question of why we say that we see the object and not the sun when we look at something that is illumined by the sun; he also answers this question in terms of causal structure and transmission of information, and he comes to formulations that are very similar to those of my paper. He talks about the "principle of constant structure" and says that the most important application of this principle is to the relation between perception and physical objects (p. 473).

Early in 1920, when I was twenty-four, I handed the thesis to Meinong. He accepted it as sufficient to qualify me for the doctor's degree, and Spitzer, the second professor on my committee, also approved it. Actually, the thesis combined two points of view. The first part developed Meinong's thinking and used his vocabulary, which I had really mastered by that time, while the second part employed simple natural-science concepts dealing with causation. I have often told how Meinong praised the first part but said that he had some reservations about the second, while Spitzer was more impressed with the second half. In any case, the thesis was accepted, and after a final examination I received my degree. My relatives were greatly baffled, because in the family I had the reputation of being a very undisciplined person who, though he sometimes had clever ideas, was always starting things but never finished them.

I had promised my father that after four years at the university I would prepare myself to earn my living. His suggestion had been that I farm some of the land that the family owned near Feistritz. It was now the spring of 1920, and the four years were up; so, one morning I walked to the agricultural school that was on the outskirts of the city, about three miles from our house. When I arrived and asked what I needed to do to be accepted as a student, they said that they did not accept students in the spring—I would have to wait until fall. I was not too disappointed, as this meant a few months' reprieve. I went into the city and bought an armful of books on cows and pigs and settled down to get some idea of what farming implied. My attitude was ambivalent: on the one hand, I had always liked to work in the open air, and I also liked animals; on the other hand, I had a feeling that my attitude toward farming was probably much too romantic and that the reality might not be so pleasant.

However, I did not get very far with the study of these books before I got an offer of a more congenial job with the provincial government of Styria. It had been decided to establish a bureau for vocational guidance, and a psychologist was needed who could devise aptitude tests for apprentices. The authorities had inquired at the university for such a person and had been given my name and address. My father accepted the change of plan, and I was soon installed in a government office as an applied psychologist.

Every year a number of boys ten or eleven years old who did not choose to continue school were accepted as apprentices to different workshops or stores. I was supposed to test these boys and to help decide where they would best fit in. I soon found that the work they were to learn was either clerical and demanded language skills or that it dealt with mechanical or spacial relations, like the job of a carpenter or locksmith. There is usually a demonstrable difference that shows rather early between these two kinds of skill, and it was not difficult to sort the boys out for the one kind of work or the other. I took pleasure in making my own tests, and I could not help being pleased when I was in Bonn, Germany, in 1960 at an international psychological meeting and saw one of them in a display of tests that were still being used in German-speaking countries and Scandinavia. I loved the occupational guidance work. I especially enjoyed the trips to smaller towns in Styria when a group of us from the bureau would go to try to impress the people with the value of what we were doing. During the day I tested boys, and in the evenings we invited the people in charge to meet with us. I displayed my little tests, and they seemed to interest everybody.

In the meantime my father and my brother, now out of the army and divorced, and I had moved again, this time from the house with the woodlot to a smaller one in town, in which I kept a little attic room where I settled and stayed off and on during the next years when I was in Graz. My brother had established a sort of factory downstairs, where he made simple radio receivers, for which there seemed to be a great demand. He had rather peculiar habits: he would often work all through the night and then sleep all morning and into the afternoon, when he would go to a downtown coffeehouse; so I did not see much of him.

I should add here that I saw less and less of Edi during the next years. By the time I went to America, he had left Graz. Neither Nora nor any of our relatives knew where he went: there was a rumor that he had gone to the Near East, either to Beirut or to Cairo. We heard that he owned a flourishing electronic business somewhere in that region, but we never really knew.

To go back to my stay in Graz. At that time there was a kind of club composed of people who were interested in natural science. I did not belong to this group, but one time they asked me to come to a meeting to tell them something about psychology. I was glad to do it. I did not talk about psychology as it was taught in a university, but I tried to explain the kind of psychology I had been thinking about during the last years and what I had read in writers like Nietzsche and Montaigne that fitted in with my ideas. The whole talk was really an autobiographical confession, especially the parts that dealt with the role that psychology might play in a person's own life. It was the first time I had tried to put these thoughts together in a coherent and orderly way, and of course, there were quite a few thoughts about interpersonal relations woven through it.

The talk was a complete flop. The people in the audience began to laugh or snicker, and before I was half through, a good many of them had left. However, this did not discourage me too much. Hans Pichler and his wife were in the audience, and they liked what I had to say. Somewhat belatedly I realize that I have not yet mentioned the Pichlers in this narrative, though they are people with whom I spent many hours during my student years and after. He was a professor at the university who mainly taught history of philosophy. He must have been about forty-five at that time; he had studied at German universities and in Paris, was widely read and sophisticated, and was a thoroughly nice person. It was a pleasure to listen to his lectures—I remember especially a series on Kant. It was unfortunate that Pichler was very hard of hearing, which made it somewhat difficult to have a real discussion with him.

His wife was Viennese, a small person who had been crippled by polio. She was very witty and had a lovely, fine face that radiated gaiety, good humor, and intelligence. For two or three years I spent an evening with them almost every week, mostly reading classics with her or listening to her tell stories while he worked in his study. I also showed her some of my little stories, which she often corrected and in doing so taught me a great deal. At about eleven,

Professor Pichler would stop his work and come out of his study to join us. I am still grateful to them for their companionship, which meant so much to me at that stage of my life and certainly made living in Graz much more pleasant for me.

YEARS OF WANDERING

In spite of the fact that I became really attached to the Pichlers and that Otto was always available for stimulating discussions, I gradually became restless in Graz and began to want a change. Meinong died soon after I had finished my work with him, and though I never considered myself close to him, I dimly felt that his death signified something like the end of another era for me. Also, the position at the vocational guidance bureau became insecure. The people in charge urged me to stay, but the postwar inflation meant that they had less and less money available for their program. It seemed natural that I thought of trying somehow to get to Berlin. Uncle Karl was now a professor there, and Doris shared his apartment and kept house for him. She wrote me about the exciting times that they had, the interesting people whom they met, visits to museums, and lectures by celebrities. I thought and thought about the possibility of going to Berlin and living with them without imposing on them financially, and finally something occurred to me. When my father was a young man and a bachelor, he was relatively well off and had indulged in various expensive hobbies, among them the buying of rare books. He gave this up after his marriage, but there were always stacks of old books in our attic, covered with dust and gradually rotting. Nobody seemed to care about them, and I thought that if I could take some of them to Berlin and sell them, I could live off the proceeds from them, at least for a few months. My father did not object to this, and Doris wrote that I should, by all means, come and stay with them. She said that she was curious about how I would fit into the Berlin scene—she had always thought of me as a person of the woods and mountains.

So, in November 1921, I set out for Berlin, which was by far the largest city I had ever lived in. After some searching, I found the apartment house where my uncle and Doris lived. Above the big entrance door there was an inscription in Latin which can be translated as "Here lives happiness—nothing bad may enter." I lived in this house off and on until the fall of 1927, and I still think of it with a warm feeling, though life during that time was not always easy for me.

I soon located the Psychological Institute, which was in the imperial palace where Kaiser Wilhelm had lived until the end of World War I, three years earlier. It was said that the institute occupied the part of the palace that was given over to the minor princesses of the family, and this seemed plausible, because there were especially long and ornate mirrors, reaching from floor to ceiling, in many of the rooms that were being used as psychological laboratories. I soon began attending lectures by Köhler and Wertheimer and seminars by Lewin.

Wertheimer was a short, intense man. He gave his lectures in one of the larger rooms of the university and was very popular with the young intellectuals of Berlin. It was always amusing to listen to him. He had a unique way both of talking and of writing. He operated by fits and starts that produced the impression that his ideas were fresh and pungent. One felt that this little man with the walrus mustache really believed what he was saying and that it must be something new since it made him so excited. One of the most enjoyable seminars I ever attended was his on the blind spot. There was a small group of ten or fifteen students, and after we had made some observations on our own blind spots, we had to suggest hypotheses to explain what we had observed. Then we had to test our hypotheses by deriving consequences from them. We had to check them then and there and make new observations to see whether they would confirm the hypotheses. It was a remarkable demonstration of the hypothetico-deductive method and, at the same time, of gestalt laws, because the way in which the blind spot appears is mainly determined by gestalt principles and not by experience. We see, not what we have "learned" to see, but what fits best.

Köhler, a younger man than Wertheimer, held the position that in America would be department chairman. He had succeeded Carl Stumpf, one of the eminent older men in psychology, who still had an office in the institute where he was working with Erich von Hornbostel on a collection of primitive music. Stumpf was the only psychologist of this older generation that I ever met personally, unless one counts Meinong among them. He and William James had been good friends; their correspondence makes delightful reading. I was glad that I had to have a conference with Stumpf in order to get a kind of stipend for a small job at the institute.

Köhler had a princely appearance. His lectures were fascinating and full of information, but he was not easy for an outsider like me to get to know. A good friend of mine told me that when he talked with Köhler, he always felt that he himself was a chimpanzee, the animal about which Köhler had written a famous book. Köhler actually had begun his academic life in physics, and he wrote a book on what he called "the physical Gestalten," in which he tried to show that the difference between physical reality and mental reality was not so great as is generally believed and that both follow structural gestalt laws.

Everybody in the institute knew the most promising student of the time, whom I shall call Binder. He was assigned the largest of the rooms set aside for students, and it was crowded with experimental apparatus. When Kurt Koffka came on a visit from Giessen, where he had become professor, the three gestalt psychologists went around to all the rooms where experiments were going on, but they always seemed to stay longest in Binder's. They came out with their eyes watering after the time they had spent looking at his demonstrations in the darkened room. The younger people even spread the story that Köhler had said that Binder knew more about perception than anybody, even Wertheimer. One had the feeling that Binder was the supreme experimenter, that he made experiments for the pure pleasure of producing complicated apparatus and looking at unusual effects. However, in the end he seemed to get more and more lost in intricacies of his own making and rather fizzled out. I do not know whether he ever got a degree, and his name does not appear once in Koffka's great book on gestalt psychology. He seems to have disappeared without leaving a trace, in spite of the high expectations with which he was seen when I was in Berlin.

I naturally found myself comparing the Berlin group—and here I mean principally Wertheimer and Köhler—with Graz's Meinong, Spitzer, and Benussi. There was, of course, a connection between the Graz school and Berlin. For one thing, Christian von Ehrenfels, whom the Berlin group recognized as one of their precursors, had been one of Meinong's students, and Wertheimer was said to have attended lectures, in his student days, by Ehrenfels at the University of Prague. Both groups were concerned with superelementary structures, the so-called *Gestalten*. Benussi and the Berliners had high regard for each other in spite of the fact that they differed in their theories about these organized units and also in their emotional attitudes toward their theories. The Berliners seemed always to be engaged in a sort of holy war against nonbelievers; they were much more belligerent and militant than the Graz group. They were fervid partisans of all the ideas that have to do with configurations and with every kind of superunit or totality. For them, the very thought of attempting to derive these noble "whole qualities" from despicable elements or pieces was unspeakably sinful, a clear sign of deplorable and corrupt thinking. They also hated the idea that mere chance could ever lead to any kind of order. Certainly, gestalt theory, as I knew it at this time in Europe, was mainly shaped by its opposition to elementarism; but later, in America, its opposition to behaviorism was much more important.

The Berlin group saw G. E. Müller as the principal advocate of a theory built on elements, bits, and crumbs. I remember a session at the psychological congress that met in Bonn in 1927, when a discussion developed between Müller and Köhler. There was this white-haired old paladin of German psychology—with a reputation almost equal to that of Wundt himself—who presented his case in a dignified and courteous way. Köhler replied, and I felt embarrassed by the sharpness of his answer.

In this connection I remember another seminar of Wertheimer's. It dealt with expression and physiognomic characters; it was held in one of the large lecture rooms of the university. One of his main points was that each person has a certain quality that Wertheimer called his *radix*—the Latin word for root. This quality will express itself in different ways: in his physiognomy; in his handwriting; in the way he dresses, moves about, talks, and acts; and also in the way he thinks, what kind of outlook he has, and if he is a scholar, in the kind of theory he builds or adopts. This was a suggestive and stimulating idea, and Wertheimer demonstrated what he meant by projecting pictures and handwriting of two people on a screen and asking the audience to match the samples of handwriting with the face of the writer. Then he gave other items to be matched. He described the one as broad-minded, generous, open, attractive, and inclined to think in holistic terms; the other, as more restricted, petty, a person who thought in terms of parts and pieces, altogether not very likable. I am not sure that many in the audience realized that the second picture was of G. E. Müller.

I also attended a series of Kurt Lewin's seminars and began to see a good deal of him. He visited me in Feistritz one summer, and we continued to be close friends until he died twenty-five years later, when we were both living in America, at that time both in Massachusetts, and visiting back and forth with our families. I showed him some of my attempts to deal with the causal structure of the environment insofar as it is relevant to perception and cognition. He suggested that we get together once a week for discussions at his house, but this did not work out, because then, as in later years, he was already overburdened with his work and all sorts of other commitments.

One ever-present problem during this time in Berlin was, of course, the necessity of earning my keep. I had sold the books from my father's attic when I arrived, but the money I got from them soon gave out. For a while I taught Latin to a little boy who had failed his final examination, but after three months he passed a second test, and the lessons came to an end. Then Lewin tried to help me. He had made himself some lampshades of very thin wood. The grain of the wood showed through when the lamps were lighted. Everybody admired them. He thought that there might be a market for them, and he suggested that I make some. I tried this, but I only sold four.

I do not remember all the different ways in which I attempted to earn enough to keep me going. At one time I returned to my old occupation of giving aptitude tests to little boys. An acquaintance who had been testing apprentices at the Borsig Locomotive Factory wanted to take time off to finish his thesis, and he asked me whether I would care to take the job on for a couple of months, and of course I was glad of the opportunity. Also, the name of Tegel, the place where the factory was located, was familiar to me, because the two Humboldts grew up there, and I had greatly enjoyed reading the extensive correspondence between Wilhelm von Humboldt and his wife. The Humboldt home was quite close to the Borsig factory, and I used to stroll around the grounds during the noon hour, though it was a rather dreary place. Nevertheless, it gave me a sort of sentimental feeling to think of the two boys, Wilhelm and Alexander, romping around under those trees.

For a while I worked for Professor Hans Rupp, who taught applied psychology at the university. He had obtained funds from the postal service for constructing tests for drivers of mail trucks, but I cannot recall much of what I did with him. Another job around that time presented me with experiences that are much more vivid in my memory: Lewin's brother owned a company that installed burglar alarms, and he asked whether I would be willing to work there as an electrician. I was glad to accept. I found this life fascinating but also exhausting. We worked in teams of two or three people, usually spending anywhere from three days to a week at one place. There was great variety in the places where we installed the alarms—at plush homes in the west end, at a big wholesale establishment in the inner city, or at a small jewelry store on the east side.

I loved diving into this ever-changing stream of life in the big city. I felt that I was gradually learning to understand and talk to all these different kinds of people. When I spoke with them, I had the feeling that I lived; when I talked with psychologists, it was to speak about life but not to live it in the same way. The atmosphere was somehow alive and stimulating. There was always a kind of intoxication that vibrated softly underneath. This work as an electrician's helper had a slightly dreamlike, romantic character. At the same time there was something exciting about it. I was living a sort of fairy-tale existence that nevertheless had an aspect of overwhelming reality. The men with whom I worked were mostly kind and well-meaning. It was natural that they soon realized that I was not an ordinary electrician's helper, and perhaps at first they had a suspicion that I had been planted among them as an informer. In any case, I was soon accepted, though they still felt that I was somehow different. I remember once, when I kissed a nice girl on the kitchen staff in one of the plutocratic houses where we were working, she looked surprised and said, *"You* should not do that!"

During this time, when I was working in one way or another to earn money, I was also trying to clear up my thoughts about all sorts of psychological problems. I was especially concerned with carrying some of the ideas of my thesis further, and in 1922 and 1923 I wrote the paper that was published in 1926 under the title *"Ding und Medium"* and in 1959 as "Thing and Medium." As I have explained, the thesis consisted of two sections, the first written in Meinong's terms, and the second using more general concepts of natural science. I now discarded the first part but expanded and elaborated the second. The main point of view of the new paper was that for the study of perception it is important to pay attention to the environmental conditions that make the perception of distant objects possible. Thus, the paper deals above all with the process that starts with the perceived object and ends with the stimuli that impinge on the sense organ (the proximal stimuli). It is not enough to say that the distal object causes the proximal stimulus. In order to understand the whole process, one has to use concepts that have to do with the coordination of manifolds, with order and disorder, with the domination of one system by another, and with constraints. Such concepts have been developed in the meantime by information theory and by cybernetics, but they were unknown in the twenties. Later, in the thirties, I showed my paper to physicists and tried to get help from them, but I met with a complete lack of understanding.

It had given me great pleasure to write that essay and to gain more insight into these relationships and networks of concepts. I find the following entry in the notes I made when I had the first inkling of the solutions to the main problems that I had been puzzling over: ''I am sometimes tired but I am at the goal. I have found what I have wished for so long, the conclusion, the great synopsis. I do not yet know what I will be able to see from this point that I have reached; and I am in no great hurry to find out. I am simply here. I stretch myself, I lie down on the grass and am happy. If I want to see more I can.''

But the notes from this time are not always so positive. I also wrote that I sometimes saw myself as an example of the unsuccessful old student: I was no longer the youngster who was full of hope. And I asked myself: ''Will I become a lonely, embittered crank? Even so, there is no other way for me. I have to make the best of the life I have chosen, to continue straight ahead. Only I must not let myself be formed by the picture that other people have of me. I must not work for the sake of external reward, I must not care whether recognition comes today or not until tomorrow. I must direct my attention to scientific problems and not to possible rewards.'' But all this did not mean that I was not extremely grateful for Lewin's support. He thought that there were some interesting new ideas in my ''Thing and Medium'' paper, and he asked whether I would like to go with him to a small gathering of people, mainly philosophers, who discussed such problems. He was sure that they would like to hear about the questions I examined in my paper. Everything would be very informal. The meeting was to be in Erlangen near Nürnberg, where the Philosophical Society had a house that served just such occasions. I accepted, of course, and we set out for Erlangen. This was in the spring of 1923.

The house turned out to be an enormous mansion, all the rooms of which were named after famous philosophers.

Lewin and I were assigned to the Aristotle Room. Besides us there were seven or eight other people, among them Rudolf Carnap and Hans Reichenbach, neither of whom was as yet well known. I especially remember Carnap's talk. At that time he was enthusiastic about the symbolic logic of Russell and Whitehead. He proceeded to explicate the statement "One and one make two" in these terms. It got more and more complicated, and when he had finished, he had filled two big blackboards with symbols. I wondered how many blackboards he would have needed to elucidate the addition involved in a simple grocery order; and I learned from this example that it is not always profitable to dig down to ultimate core concepts. I have great respect for explication and analysis; I often try it myself, and I find that it usually serves to simplify problems. But I also find that analysis can go too far and that it then has the effect of complicating things. Cleverness also has to be used with discretion. In the course of these meetings I gave a talk on my ideas about certain problems of cognition, and the discussions afterwards strengthened my feeling that it was worthwhile to develop them further.

I may add a postscript to my account of the meeting, a note which concerns the building in which we stayed. There was usually a resident secretary of the Philosophical Society living there. About a month after our meeting, I believe it was, he began to notice that there was some sand on his desk every morning. He was puzzled until he looked at the ceiling and saw a little crack just above the desk. He called the people who were responsible for the upkeep of the building. They investigated and told him that he had to get out right away. Erlangen was an old beer town, and the medieval cellars that were under the house, but no longer used, were caving in. The whole house used by the Philosophical Society disappeared within a short time, crumbling into the old cellar. I always thought that there was a philosophical message in this event, but maybe it was just as well that I never found out what it was.

But to go back to the tale of my job experiences as I tried to earn my living and continue some kind of intellectual life in Berlin: After a couple of months the glamor of my life as a burglar-alarm electrician was beginning to wear off. I was tired out and beginning to feel that I was caught in a dead end, when there appeared a new prospect that seemed worth considering. It was Doris who suggested it. She had a friend who worked in an orphanage in the region of the Harz Mountains, about a hundred miles from Berlin. There had been a famous educator named Hermann Lietz who had founded a number of boarding schools in Germany. They were usually located in beautiful places, often in old castles, and were supposed to provide a broad education and to produce generally cultured people, in contrast to the gymnasium, which he felt stressed mere book learning too much. But since these schools were rather expensive, only an elite could attend them, and Lietz wanted to found a school for poor children, especially orphans, with some of the same features. The school that Doris knew about in Veckenstedt was the result. It was located in the flat country, with plains extending to the horizon in the north and mountains rising sharply to the south. There were forty or fifty children, ranging in age from ten to sixteen years, and ten or fifteen adults, all living in an old farmhouse, which had served as a mill driven by a little brook.

The head of this orphanage very kindly agreed to take a chance with such an irregular person as I seemed to be, and in March of 1924 I set out to learn something about still another setting. Soon after I had arrived, I was asked to help spade up a small vegetable plot. When I found my way to the plot, there was a friendly, elderly man already working there. I had seen him around and knew that he must be Gustav. The children had told me about him, that he often came to visit the school and that he told them wonderful stories but would not allow adults to listen in. I gradually came to know him and his history. He was Gustav Naumann and belonged to the Naumann family of publishers. They had put out Nietzsche's first books, and once, when Gustav was a young man, they had commissioned him to try to locate some unpublished manuscripts by Nietzsche that were believed still to exist. It was assumed that they must have been left in places where Nietzsche had lived in northern Italy. Gustav had luck and found the manuscript of the *Will to Power* in Turin. I also heard that Gustav was a well-known writer of boys' books. In his room he had a large autographed photograph of Hindenburg, who seemed to have been a great admirer of these books. Gustav was a restless spirit—he would stay only two or three weeks at the orphanage; then he would disappear, and nobody would seem to know where he had gone.

My next job was to help Herr Dietrich build a wall. I had never met anyone like Herr Dietrich before. He did not belong to the school but came from a neighboring village. He lived in a world of medieval sagas that he would tell in great detail and with complete confidence in their truth. He really believed that an age-old, hoary king still lived somewhere underground and that we, the present generation, would see his resurrection. He would come in a great storm, and Dietrich described in biblical language how this new over-lord would cleanse the land and drive out corruption and baseness. I can well believe that Herr Dietrich a few years later would become a fanatic Nazi, though I never heard him speak of Hitler. At least he offered a contrast to the Berlin electricians. Talking with him, one felt in touch with the prehistoric world or with deep layers of a heroic age about which I had read. And all this seemed to fit the landscape. I only had to look out the window to see the Brocken, the highest mountain in the Harz, which is associated with endless myths and legends. It is the place where, we are told, the witches and sorcerers held their yearly conclaves and where Faust and Mephisto visited them.

Besides spading the vegetable garden and helping the bricklayer, I was supposed to do a number of different jobs during the summer. One chore, which was my responsibility all the time I lived at the school, was to keep the electrical installation that supplied light for the school functioning. As I have mentioned, the farmhouse in which all of us lived had also served as a mill with a regular millwheel that was turned by the little brook. This wheel now drove an electrical generator, and the electricity was stored in a number of old-fashioned batteries. All this had to be kept clean and in good working order: it was important to watch out that the current did not flow in the wrong direction. If this happened, the batteries would be using the energy stored in them to turn the wheel whenever the brook was dry. Then I helped with farm work such as cutting hay, bringing it in with a little wagon pulled by a donkey, and storing it in the loft of the barn. I also did some teaching, giving classes in physics and swimming. For two weeks I was busy picking cherries in a beautiful old orchard. And since I seemed to get on with the donkey, I was often sent with the wagon to do errands in the village. Also, there were special occasions in which I participated. One of the teachers was a musician who prepared a simple performance of the *Magic Flute*. He narrated the plot, and I played the piano to accompany the arias and choral numbers that the children sang.

One event of the summer is especially fresh in my memory. Early one morning—it may have been four o'clock—someone knocked on my door and whispered: "The bailiff is here looking for good swimmers. Can you come? A man has been drowned in the pond." I hurriedly dressed and went with one of the teachers to follow the officer. At the edge of the pond there were people from the forest rangers' headquarters nearby. They told us how they had heard a man shout: "Don't bother with the boat. I can swim without it." So they went on with their work, then after a while, they began to look about to see where he was and could not find him. We talked about the condition of the pond—the water was so muddy that we could not see the bottom. Then maybe ten people held hands so as to make a chain, and half wading, half swimming, we tried to explore the pond, expecting any moment to locate the missing man. We had no success. We finally gave up and gathered in a little cabin, where some women served hot coffee. The nearness of death had loosened our restraints; we talked about religion, philosophy, and the riddle of life; and we felt close to each other as we saw the early rays of the rising sun. Later in the day the body was found.

I should try to describe the general atmosphere of the home. Zollmann, the director, was a complicated person. I often had the feeling that he took special pleasure in improving others; therefore he corrected them, something that in itself was only praiseworthy. But in order to do this he had to be constantly looking for the shortcomings and errors of the people around him, which he was very ingenious at finding. He often aroused my antagonism. My defense was quiet humor, which suggested a refusal to take him seriously. I was always polite, but I did not let myself get involved in discussing his judgments of myself or others. I must have been quite annoying to him at times.

At the same time, there were occasions when I sincerely admired him. For instance, I remember the way he handled one small disturbance at the home. To quiet things down, he talked about the incident at the next weekly assembly when all the children and adults got together. He began by describing what had happened: one little boy who came from the city had used an obscene word. Another child had slapped him, and the case had been taken to Zollmann, who discussed the matter in a sensible way with the two children. He assumed that it was all settled, but one girl who had heard the word kept thinking about it and repeated it to a special friend of hers. And so the story of a secret, forbidden word got around. The other children began to feel very superior to the naughty people who would use such a word, and a little boy who repeated it without having the least idea of what it meant was beaten up. By this time, everybody in the house was upset. Zollmann's talk changed the whole situation. It was remarkable how he calmed the disorder without punishing anybody.

I suppose that the general atmosphere of the home was very much shaped by the memory of Lietz, the founder, who had been Zollmann's teacher. What was stressed was a loathing of luxury and of undisciplined laxity. Work in itself was held to be one of the great values. If play came in at all, it should be in the form of strenuous competitive sport. The person who could control his own body and who did not wince at pain or try to avoid exertion was to be admired.

But in spite of this emphasis on discipline, the atmosphere was not authoritarian. The director and the teachers tried to train the children to be independent, to assume responsibility, and to act on their own initiative. They were also expected to be able to cope with an emergency. Once, everybody—teachers and children—set out to climb a high peak of the mountain wall that we could see from the school. When we reached the foot of our mountain, a group of boys started to scramble over the rocks along the path. I could see that they had had no experience with climbing rocks and that they went at it in a clumsy fashion. I remembered travelers from the plains who tried to climb around in the Alps without knowing how to do it and who were brought back on stretchers. I asked Zollmann whether the boys should be turned loose on the rocks this way, and he said, "Boys must be risked." He meant that they had to find out for themselves how to face danger.

At the school I often saw a small boy, maybe ten years old, with a big ox, plowing a field all by himself. It seemed that some of these children looked curiously adult and old, as though worn down by care. There was little play or laughter around, and I felt as though I was living among little old shriveled men and women. I slowly came to realize the difficulties that an institution like this orphanage had to contend with. The original plan of having a school for poor children that would be supported by the work of teachers and pupils seemed plausible and a good idea. By working together on a farm with their teachers, the children would learn a great deal that they would never learn in a schoolroom. But in practice there seemed to be a number of troubling weaknesses. I began to feel that the house was not a healthy place for a person to be in. Few of the workers stayed any length of time. The teachers were so busy with practical farm work that they had little time to read or prepare lessons. Therefore, in the end, they were really farm workers who were mere dilettantes at teaching. All this bothered me quite a bit. When Doris came once to visit, she was troubled by my tired and worn appearance. I told her that I could not go on with the life there much longer, and in October I decided to leave. I had been at the home since March, when the little stream was still covered with ice, and now everything was settling down for another winter. I was longing for solitude, for my little room in Graz, where I could go out without being right away in the midst of people, and for the long mountain walks of Styria, which I was free to take on my own whenever I wanted to. I was sure that I would never be able to adjust to a life in which I was constantly surrounded by people. I looked back with nostalgia to the days of writing my thesis in Graz, or to Berlin, when I was working on the theory of perception. I could not forget the wonderful feeling of liberation when I had struggled through a thicket of perplexities and had solved a puzzling problem. I was no longer eager for new experiences and new surroundings. I had been through so much that was new during the last years. I felt that my mind was stuffed with a mass of undigested nourishment. All this needed to be worked over and clarified. So, I said goodby to all the people at the orphanage—the children and the teachers. It touched me to feel how warm and friendly they were in parting, and I believed that they were sincere when they said that they would miss me. Even Zollmann dropped his director's role as he wished me good luck. I harnessed the little donkey, whom I had come to love, for the last time to go to the station, and one teacher accompanied me. I started on the trip to Austria.

It was a long train ride, and I had lots to think about. What would become of me now? Would I return to Graz as a failure? I could not accept that thought when I looked back on the wealth of impressions that I had hoarded up—it couldn't be all for nothing. In any case, I was not going directly to Graz but would stop off in Vienna with relatives. That would postpone the final decision. Gusti (pronounced Goo'stee)—a bachelor second cousin and close friend who was the grandson of one of the brothers of Moriz the dentist—lived there. In age he was closer to my father's generation than to mine, but Doris and the Vienna cousins and I always thought of him as belonging more to us younger people. When we were at Feistritz, he joined in our games and walks. His work was with the government bank. He made his home with two elderly spinster aunts, nieces of the dentist. One of these aunts, Julia Heider, we loved dearly. She was still full of fun and energy, while her sister, Lina, who was ten years older, was more sedate. I usually stayed with Gusti and the aunts when I passed through Vienna. This time, Gusti took me for a walk, and we climbed one of the towers of St. Stephan's Cathedral. Halfway up the narrow stairway he said something that brought about a profound change in my life for the next years and probably influenced my whole future. He offered to give me a small monthly allowance—not much, but enough so that I was no longer under constant pressure to earn my living. He made the offer without tying any conditions to it, and I was deeply grateful. I may not have appreciated its full significance at the moment, but now, looking back, I know that it came at a critical time in my life. I do not know what would have become of me without it.

I traveled on to Graz with a lighter heart. In the meantime there had been an important change in my father's life. He had married a young woman, not quite as old as I, and in many ways a rare and admirable person. Her name was Mizi. She was now my stepmother—someone with whom I and the relatives who gathered in the summers felt very comfortable. My father had regained some of his youth, and whenever I was in Graz during the next years, I had supper with him and Mizi in their apartment once or twice a week.

Mizi had grown up in the Youth Movement and was always engaged in charitable activities of one sort or another. She was cheerful—just the right kind of person for my father. He liked a life of simple values. He hated big-city ostentation, social class pretensions, and the loud vulgarity of many rich people. He was greatly interested in many of the religious and scientific questions that were also of importance to the people of the Youth Movement, so he and Mizi had much to talk about. In time they had two daughters, Reingard and Gertraud, who still live in Graz and whom I see whenever I get there. Gradually my father noticed that I seemed to have an income from some source that he did not know about. I did not explain this, because Gusti had asked me not to, and my father did not ask me directly where the money came from. I am sure that he was worried and perhaps a little annoyed that I seemed to get away with continuing my apparently aimless, lazy life and that I still avoided making a start on a steady job. He probably felt that it could only end in my being a loafer the rest of my life, and he may have blamed himself for being too easygoing with me as I grew up. I still have a letter from Doris in which she told me that he had written her that he wondered who was supporting me and that he was not altogether grateful to that person for encouraging me in my ways. He obviously suspected that she or her father was helping me, and he wanted them to know that he felt it was a mistaken kindness.

During my stay in Berlin, Otto had become involved in a relationship that gradually came to have more and more significance for him as well as for me. It may have been already before I left Graz for Berlin that he wrote an article on synesthesia for a popular science magazine. This term refers to cases in which the stimulation that ordinarily belongs to one sense modality produces the experience usually identified with a different modality. An example would be the seeing of a flash of yellow light on hearing a trumpet blast. There are quite a few people who have had this sort of experience, and Otto wanted to find out more about it. He included in his article a request that anyone who had experienced this phenomenon should write to him. I remember the afternoon when he showed me a pile of letters that he had received. He picked one up and asked, "What do you think of this one?" It was from a young woman who lived in a Czechoslovakian village near the Riesengebirge. I read it and was impressed by it. I asked him, "What are you going to do with it?" "Oh, I'll answer it," he said. And that is how the girl whose name was Gerti entered the lives of Otto and of me.

Soon Otto and Gerti began to correspond. She lived with her grandmother on a large estate which Gerti managed. She invited Otto to visit them, and while I was in Berlin, he often stayed with them. They urged me to stop off on my trips between Graz and Berlin. I did so and thus got acquainted with Gerti. She was an entrancing creature, full of vitality and gaiety, with an insatiable curiosity about everything. She enjoyed long discussions with Otto. They had obviously become fond of each other, but only as friends. I do not believe that they ever thought of anything more. Gerti soon realized that I had a great yearning for a peaceful place where I could work without money troubles. She said, in a tentative way, that there were lots of quiet rooms in their big house and that I would be welcome anytime to stay there for a while. She would be quiet as a mouse and would not disturb me. I did not respond right away, but a year or so later I wrote her from Graz to ask whether it would be all right with her grandmother and her for me to come. She answered right away, and in March 1925, I found myself settled for a time in the big house in Czechoslovakia.

This house was situated on the outskirts of a little village. I soon got to know the region as I took walks in all directions. It reminded me of the landscape around Feistritz, where I had spent so many summers. It also had great variety, and one could find walks fitting whatever mood one happened to be in. There was a path through a narrow, dark, wooded valley, or one along a ridge with changing views, or still another one through thick woods with high fir trees or grassland with scattered groves. Or one could follow a little stream up one side of a mountain to find the spring that nourished it. Each choice offered its own peculiar temper and complexion, whether sweet or harsh, flashy or modest. Not far from the house and lying within the estate, there was a baroque wilderness area, a maze of fantastic and bizarre rock formations, that was mentioned in every guide book as one of the sights of the region. I was told that it was like a perilous labyrinth and that Gerti was the only person who knew its paths—anyone else who tried to explore it would get hopelessly lost.

Gerti not only knew her way along all these paths; she knew the flowers and animals that were to be found along them. She was like a pagan deity, living off the richness of nature—a wood nymph or a water sprite. I had never known anyone who responded so sensitively to everything that nature offers. In my family there were several who had great interest in plants. But usually each plant represented an exercise in botany, in determining its name in terms of Linnaeus. Once it had been correctly classified, it would be pressed between sheets of blotting paper, and that was that. For Gerti, every plant had an expressive face and spoke to

her, complained about food and water, or purred content-
edly in the sunlight. She knew right away if a wild animal
was not behaving in its usual way, how to treat a sick
animal, and how to console one that was uncomfortable.

Gerti and her grandmother did not have much social
life. Gerti had a sister, who had married in Silesia and whom
she visited from time to time. Her closest friend was a
woman who lived on a neighboring estate, four or five miles
away. Eventually I learned that this woman had grown up in
Innsbruck and that her closest friend during her childhood
had been Doris. "That is too much," I said to myself. "Is
some fate weaving a net for me?"

When I began this life in Czechoslovakia, I naturally
thought of the possibility that I might fall in love with Gerti.
However, I thought that I was safe. As I told myself: "I am
the man dedicated to science. I cannot allow myself to think
about love and marriage and children with all the complica-
tions and consequences of these relationships." And I
thought that my attachment to Doris, my "beloved sister,"
would keep me safe from entanglements with other women.
Also, I had some reservations about Gerti. To state it bluntly,
I was not sure that she was a person I could entirely trust. In
spite of her fascinating charm, I often felt something about
her that troubled me. She told me long stories that I was sure
were partly fabricated, and I suffered as I tried in vain to
settle my doubts.

I could not help comparing her with Doris, with whom
it was sometimes difficult to get on. Doris could be can-
tankerous and shrewish, and almost every year we had at
least one tremendous fight. But it never lasted; when it was
over, she would come back to me sweetly and laugh and say
that in spite of our disagreements, I was the only one with
whom she could really share her troubles. To me, her life
was an open book, transparent and understandable, without
any shady corners. I had told Gerti very early that I was not
the marrying kind. I should have left at that point, for I

became sure that she wanted more. But she insisted that she would forget me as soon as the train on which I would decide to leave had pulled out of the station.

In June 1925 I went back to Graz. I will always be grateful to Gerti and her grandmother for the haven they gave me that year. I saw Gerti several times later. Once in 1925 she and her grandmother made a trip to Yugoslavia, and I saw them there when I was on my way to Florence later in the year. I soon felt that Gerti was getting more and more dependent on me, but since I could not imagine having a real relationship with her, I said that we would have to say goodby and not even write each other any more. She accepted this, and a year or so later she married. Otto, who had kept more closely in touch with her, gave me to understand that the man was beneath Gerti in every respect. I saw her again later, when she came to Hamburg while I was living there. I pitied her for wasting herself in this way. It is now more than fifty years since that spring in Czechoslovakia. Gerti died long ago, but I still find myself in a sober and pensive mood when I think of her. The words of Goethe come to my mind when he makes the harp player in *Wilhelm Meister* complain to the heavenly powers that they lead us into life and let us become guilty.

Gusti's stipend now gave me a modest security, but I still did not seem to settle down to productive psychological research in my room above my brother's radio business in Graz. I became restless, and since I had always wanted to try living in a place where a language other than German was spoken, I decided to spend a few months in Florence. I knew a little Italian.

It was on my way to Florence in November 1925 that I stopped off in Padua and saw Benussi for the last time. I have only a dim memory of the frail, sad, tired man I found sitting in a big, dark room. He seemed very glad to see a student from his days in Graz, and he asked me many questions about the psychologists in Berlin.

It was cold and rainy when I arrived in Florence and tried to find a place to live. I was told that there was a room to let in one of the streets behind the cathedral. I went there, entered a dark hall in a house that was perhaps four hundred years old, and climbed up to the second floor. A small, elderly woman with a hunched back opened the door. When I inquired about a room, she answered in a sullen, unfriendly voice that she had only one tiny chamber that could be rented. Soon another gray-haired woman appeared; this one had a soft, plump face and was as amiable and sweet in her manner as her partner was grim. Her whole body and all her gestures expressed a desire to be helpful and to please: her head swayed to and fro in a gracious manner, and when she spoke, she stretched her words to a melodious sing-song that reminded me of the meowing of a friendly cat. We soon came to an agreement about the price, and the next day I moved in.

The two women were sisters. The little hunchback was an old spinster. Her name was Sara. The friendly one was a widow who had taught school. Her name was Lisa, and she was clearly mistress of the little household, while Sara was the slave who had to work from early morning until late at night. When winter started, a rather severe one for Florence, Lisa stayed in bed most of the day, and Sara had to wait on her. Sara spent her time running to and fro, shopping, cooking, and cleaning the rooms. She seemed to become more and more skinny as the winter progressed, and her dull eyes almost disappeared in their dark cavities. Every so often Lisa would appear, well rested and cheerful, complaining about the miserable weather and the deficiencies of her sister. "You must have noticed," she said, "that Sara is not quite right in the head. It is not her fault. She is a poor creature."

However, one could not say that Lisa was a heartless egoist. She was generally amiable and helpful to the people about her, and she was very popular with her old pupils.

She always had a friendly word for me, and she tried to make my stay in Florence as pleasant as possible. Once she said to me: "You see, I have a son in Rome. He is like you; he also lives with strangers. I like to treat you well so that my son will also be treated well."

On the other hand, the poor harassed Sara was always ill-natured and peevish. She was a weak and helpless soul. The amount of work expected of her far exceeded her limited mental and physical capacity. When she set the table, she ran back and forth between the kitchen and the dining room, carrying each plate and fork separately. She was always shuffling around in her slippers, muttering to remind herself of what she had to do next. As far as she was concerned, I was just an addition to her daily toil and drudgery, a new worry added to all the others, and she was trying as far as she could to get rid of me by being unpleasant. I had arranged to have my breakfast and luncheon at the house, which led to difficulties, because I never knew when Sara would bring the luncheon. It might be at one o'clock, or it might be two or three hours later. When I asked her whether we could agree on a time, she said: "Well, if you really want everything exactly on time, you should go to a hotel or find some old, pedantic people. We do not live so exactly by the clock. With us there is always youthful confusion." In the end I adapted myself to this confusion as far as possible.

In the evening after supper, Sara would disappear, and Lisa would come out of her seclusion and sit at the table downstairs in the living room, reading or writing, with a flickering candle as the only illumination. It was often chilly, and she would hold her hands over a *caldaio*, a little wire basket that held glowing pieces of charcoal. I often sat beside her, and she would try to make me familiar with the beauties of the Italian language. She read pieces that she liked especially, or we read Dante together and she would explain passages that I did not understand. Her genuine enthusiasm for the language was very attractive. I am still grateful to her for trying to educate me.

I had to recognize that in many ways Lisa was a generous person and did not at all fit the role that she seemed to play in relation to Sara. My Italian was not flexible enough for me to inquire more deeply into this domestic situation without hurting Lisa's feelings. But sometimes I wondered whether it was not possible that Sara herself shaped her life so that she could feel mistreated.

I can mention an incident that showed Lisa's generosity. One evening, it may have been about ten o'clock, when I was taking a stroll in the inner city, a man asked me in broken German if I happened to be Austrian or German. I replied that I was, and he asked if I knew where he could find lodging for the night. His clothing was neat, though rather poor, and there was something appealing and interesting about him. I learned that he was a Russian dental technician who had traveled widely and was now looking for a job. In Italy he had been sent from one city to the next, and he complained that Italians thought that any man without a job was a scoundrel. I invited him to come with me to see whether my landlady would fix up a bed for him for the night. He was happy to accept, and I introduced him to Lisa. She welcomed him cordially, and she agreed to let him stay overnight, though by now it was getting toward midnight. She praised me for being so kindhearted, and she told me that I should always bring a poor person who was homeless to her.

She brought out a warm supper and tried to make the stranger comfortable. He and Lisa were soon exchanging views on the meaning of life. He was rather dejected and said, "It is best to be dead; then one has peace and quiet." Lisa became all excited and said: "No, no. After death begins a fuller and more complete life." "Perhaps, perhaps," the Russian answered. "But down here it is not very nice. Everybody is miserable." And so they went on discussing death and happiness. Just then a moth fell into the soup, and he said: "See here, how it dies. Happy moth!" But at this moment the moth got out again and flew away. Lisa laughed triumphantly and said: "You see, a new life. A new and better life! Don't give up hope too soon!"

Later he said: "Yes, I love pictures and art, and everything that is so beautiful here in Italy. But when you are miserable and have no home, no money, and no friends, then all this beauty counts for nothing. It is shallow and superficial. Misery makes us look beneath the surface, and all that matters is whether you find a compassionate heart." Then he went on: "I often think of a saying I heard from someone—'Money lost, little lost; honor lost, much lost; courage lost, everything lost'—and that is really true." He quoted what was a piece of common wisdom, which gained a peculiar poignancy coming from a man who had walked the length of Italy and found no work and little help all along the way.

Lisa fixed a bed for him on the living room floor, and all of us soon retired. He was not there when we got up the next morning. He must have left early, but he had folded the bed linen neatly before he went.

While I was in Florence, I went, almost every evening, to a café on Cathedral Square, where a group of painters, mostly German, used to gather. I came to know one of them more closely, whom I shall call Ernst. He himself was not a painter, but he was widely informed in many fields. He had a Ph.D. from Würzburg in art history and psychology. It was very stimulating to listen to him talk about his ideas. At that time he had no regular job but was earning a little by cataloguing the extensive library, mostly English and American books, that belonged to the widow of a recently deceased American writer. Since I was not endowed with the gift of prophecy, I could not have guessed that this American had been a distant relative, by an earlier marriage, of the American girl who would become my wife a few years later.

Ernst always seemed somehow to live on the edge of sanity, and one felt that one might, at any moment, lose contact with him. He was steeped in Eastern wisdom and had all kinds of notions about the occult. In addition he had a very high opinion of himself, and he suffered from a feeling that he was the object of persecution. As he told it, there were several groups trying to catch him, perhaps to torment him, especially the Freemasons, the Jesuits, and sometimes the fascists. He had only to go out on the street to see how they communicated with each other by secret signs. So far, he had always eluded them, although they were very clever and powerful; but he would never submit: "There must always be a few people who hold the Grail high. Nietzsche had to suffer as I do." To strengthen his mental powers he practiced meditation.

Once I went with Ernst to the Medici Chapel to look at the statues by Michelangelo. There are four figures at the feet of the two Medici princes. One pair is usually called Day and Night; the other, Dawn and Evening. Ernst said that they represented the four basic forms of matter—the figure of Day being the first form, the body of man as such, and that is why that figure lies there as if it were dead. The figure of Night is meant to be the second form of matter, with its carnal appetite, and is symbolized by a sensual woman. In this way he explained all the hidden meanings that he believed Michelangelo had depicted in the chapel. Another time he said that Michelangelo's mural of the *Last Judgment* in the Sistine Chapel is the biggest insult the Church ever had to swallow, because the Apollonian picture of Christ is outside of the Palladium and of the Grail, which means that the Church has not yet reached its goal. He did not answer when I asked what "outside of the Palladium" meant; and when I asked further, "Where is the Grail today?" he said it was better not to talk of some things, giving me to understand that he knew very well where it was.

Though is was a rather cold winter in Florence, I took walks in the surrounding hills. One sunday I climbed Mount Morello, a mountain to the north of the city, about three thousand feet high. The weather was relatively benign, and I expected to find quite a few people enjoying the outdoors. However, as I climbed up the nice path, I saw nobody at all except some people in the distance who looked like hunters or shepherds. When I came to the top of the mountain, a man with a cane and a hat that was tied to his head with a scarf appeared from the other side. We greeted each other; he expressed his admiration of the view and named all the mountains around. He went on: "I love nothing so much as to take walks in this region. I know each path, each mountain, and each house. I am an old man, sixty years old, but my legs are still young. This is my automobile," he said as he patted his thighs. "I got up at five o'clock and walked all the way." I spoke of my surprise that there were not more people from Florence on the mountain to enjoy the view. "Oh, I know," he said. "I often urge the young people to climb Mount Morello—to follow the foolish old man—for that is what they call me. Down there they know about me and my obsession—but they prefer to go to the movies. They have no idea how beautiful it is here, how clear the air, and how wide the view over the land. They are lazy and stay down there in the fog. I go into the mountains, and when I do meet anybody, it is always a foreigner. Perhaps I am not a true Florentine."

On the way home he told me about himself. He had been a locomotive engineer but was now retired. "Thirty-five years of work, and what work! Thirty-five years with a black face!" He led me along a beautiful path down to the city, and when we parted, he thanked me profusely for having been such good company. I could not help speculating about his appearance and manner and wondering whether I would ever have met such a man in the hills around Graz. I would certainly have found many more people hiking or strolling there, but I would hardly have found a locomotive engineer who would have expressed his enjoyment of the scenery in language as pure and beautiful as this Florentine's.

I spent a good deal of my time in Florence visiting the museums. I had some acquaintance with the museums in Vienna, Munich, and Berlin, and I had attended lectures on the history of art. One course that I will never forget was given by the great Heinrich Wölfflin in Munich. In Florence I went almost every day to one of the museums. I was able to do this in spite of my limited income because the art historian of the University of Graz had written a recommendation for me, and I was thus able to get a free pass to all of them.

It was in Florence that I began to think more about art appreciation. One might think that all one has to do is to stand before a picture and look at it in order to have the same experience that a schooled connoisseur has when he looks at it. The stimuli reaching the eye are the same. Even if one grants that the connoisseur has more information about the artist and his times, it would seem plausible that he would see the same picture as the layman. The more I thought about the problems of art appreciation, the more I realized how little I "understood" many of the pictures—for instance, those belonging to the early Renaissance. And to use the word "understand" in this connection does not do justice to the case, because we are dealing, not with rational understanding, but with a kind of responding that makes it possible to enjoy all the virtues of a piece of art and that only indirectly has to do with intellectual knowledge concerning the genesis of the picture.

I had given much thought to visual perception when I wrote my thesis, but then I was mainly concerned with its cognitive aspects and with the problem of how information about things in space reaches the retina. But when one tries to attain a greater understanding of art appreciation, a new element comes in that is only indirectly related to the intellectual aspect of getting to know one's environment. This new element has to do with attitudes about values and with like and dislike.

As I strolled through the museums, I got more and more the feeling that I was surrounded by great riches without being able fully to enjoy them and that what made it impossible for me to benefit from them was not a lack of any kind of intellectual knowledge but rather a deficiency in the education of the eye. To try to improve one's understanding of art by reading about it is somewhat like trying to learn to skate or ride a bicycle from a book. The only way to train the eye is to look at pictures over and over. It was this conviction that made me spend so much time in the cold galleries of Florence that winter.

On the last day of my stay I was mostly with Ernst. There was a German institute for art history in the city, and Ernst had somehow gotten into trouble with its director. He was furious and took the affair very seriously. He said that the director had insulted him, that his honor was at stake, and that he had to do something to regain the respect of the community of art historians. He even talked of a "court of honor," with Bernard Berenson, then dean of the art historians living around Florence, presiding. I thought that he greatly exaggerated the importance of the affair, though I don't remember now what actually had happened between him and the director. I do, however, have a vivid memory of sitting for hours in a café, trying to reason with him. In the end, I believe I convinced him to some extent; but when I left, he sat there looking altogether dismal, with the hope of playing a hero's role at a court of honor greatly diminished. He said that he would leave Florence soon and go to Berlin. I gave him the address of my uncle and Doris. Later I heard that he had stayed with them for a while. When my uncle left Berlin, Ernst went to some of Doris's friends and then disappeared into the Baltic regions. Doris wrote that they called him the *Unglückswurm* (the worm of misfortune) and that what, at first, gave an impression of depth in Ernst was really just his own superstitions. I may mention that he will reappear in this story at a later time and under quite different circumstances.

After this long session in the café, I hurried off to say goodby to Lisa and Sara. Lisa was very touching; she asked me whether there was anybody in Austria with whom I could read Dante. Even Sara tried to give me a friendly smile and wished me luck. Then I ran to the station with my bag, once more crossing the square in front of the cathedral, and took the night train for Graz. This was in January 1926.

I think it must have been when I was in Graz at this time that I had a memorable encounter. One afternoon, when I happened to pass the physics building at the university, I saw a notice on the door announcing that someone with the name of Alfred Wegener would give a talk that evening on "The Geology of Continents." At that time there were rather few scientific lectures of general interest at the university; so I decided to go. When I went into the building, I found that the room where the lecture was to be given was a small one with only a few chairs, and there was only one other person there, obviously waiting for the lecturer to appear. He soon came, accompanied by a woman and an elderly man, and talked in a very interesting way about what has become known as the theory of continental drift. I was fascinated, both by the man himself and by his theories, and I stayed after the lecture, talking with him and the two people with him, who were his wife and her father. He said that they had come to Graz that winter from Germany because his father-in-law was not well, and they hoped that the milder climate of southern Austria would help him. They invited me to go to see them, but somehow I never did. A few years later I read in the paper that Wegener had died on a trip through Greenland.

That same summer, in 1926, I went to Italy again, this time to Naples. Uncle Karl, Doris's father, had retired as a professor at Berlin and had gone to Naples to work at the aquarium, where he had friends among the zoologists. Doris had gone with him. She had gotten into a difficult situation with a married man who was also a visitor at the aquarium.

She always wrote me about her adventures. I had received a desperate letter, in which she said that she had nobody to talk to about her problem and asked me to come to Naples for a while. She said that her father, who was usually a kind and considerate man, refused to involve himself in this matter. He had told her: "All your trouble is your own doing. You went into this mess with your eyes open, and you have to find a way out."

I packed up and started south. Since my train stopped for half an hour in Florence, I got off and raced along the familiar streets toward the cathedral. Along the way I met one of the men whom I had gotten to know during the winter, and he told me that practically everybody of the old crowd that used to get together at the café in the evening had left. I went back to the train and, without stopping off at Rome, traveled on and arrived the next morning at Naples, where my uncle met me at the station.

Uncle Karl and Doris had rented a beautiful little house at the eastern end of the Vomero, the hill behind Naples. It was a very comfortable place with a magnificent view of the Gulf of Naples and Mount Vesuvius from the roof, where it was pleasant to sit in the evenings. Doris and I usually went up there after supper to talk about her predicament. I soon found out that it was a rather hopeless case. I could not do much for her except to listen sympathetically as she tried to get a clearer understanding of herself and her situation by talking about it. Now, when I look back more than fifty years to that summer, and when Doris has been dead for more than forty years, I believe that during these weeks in Naples there emerged a subtle change in my relationship to her. I had become less dependent on her, and my feeling for her no longer had the quality of an adolescent crush that endowed her with an awesome power over my happiness. It had become a more even fondness, a genuine caring for a very dear sister.

I would like to insert here the account of an event that I observed that summer. It was something that happened very rapidly, in maybe less than five seconds, but I have never forgotten it. It always seemed to me to be an instructive example of the way in which the relations among a small group of persons can be intertwined. I will introduce the persons taking part in the scene only in terms of their roles: Several people are sitting at a table having tea. There are a man, his wife, and their daughter. Then there is a woman with whom the man is having an affair. Besides these four, there are two other people who take no part in the event that I am describing. The man and the woman he loves are hungry for some kind of personal contact with each other, if it is only to exchange a glance; at the same time, the jealous wife wants just as much to prevent that contact. She has her eyes glued on the two so as not to miss their slightest move. Then, as it happened, the daughter says something that attracts her mother's attention for a moment. The two who are in love see that, and they exchange a quick glance of comfort in their unhappy situation. The wife catches their glance and glowers furiously at the pair, who right away look at their plates.

I suppose the fact that this situation seemed immediately so full of meaning and that I never forgot it is connected with my attempts to think about interpersonal structures involving more than two persons and that I already had some dim notion of the rationale underlying such interactions. In order to prevent a misunderstanding that might come about in too quick an application of this example to some of my later theorizing, I should add that the incident is not an example of simple balance: it deals with monopolistic or exclusive connections and sentiments where there is no transivity.

To continue my narrative: The region around Naples was very rich in beautiful scenes. My uncle and Doris had stayed there off and on for years, and they showed me many of their favorite spots. Uncle Karl often selected a view and settled down to paint, while Doris and I climbed around on

73

the neighboring hills. Every so often I took off by myself to visit sights that they did not especially care to see again. Besides Pompeii I went to see other remains of classical antiquity, especially the Greek temples at Paestum. I will not try to describe these temples. It was as though I were confronted by an overwhelming presence; I had the feeling that I could not do justice to it, as if I had a book in my hand which I knew was of tremendous importance but which, for some reason, I could not read.

Once I walked up Mount Vesuvius at night when the moon was full. The volcano had looked very inviting when I looked at it from the roof of our house. But on a weekday and at night, I rather expected to be the only person who would think of climbing it. I took a streetcar to the foot of the mountain. To my surprise, it was full of people who also wanted to spend the evening on Vesuvius. The closer we came to Resina, the place where one starts the climb, the more people joined us. As I walked up the path from the railway, I fell in with a group of young people with whom I stayed all the way to the top. The view of the city, the gulf, and the islands was incredibly beautiful in the light of the full moon. One almost had a feeling of oversatiation, like eating too much of a dessert that is very sweet. We came to the edge of the crater at two or three in the morning. Everybody rested there for a while before the walk down.

The Neapolitan dialect, with its compressions and abbreviations, was much harder for me to understand than the clear Tuscan language of Florence. When I think of those summer days in Naples, I have a dim memory of noisy movements of masses of people, a surging of multitudes with much laughter and cheerful, restless activity. People wanted to get in touch; everywhere one felt that they had a need for human contact. And this seemed especially strong when a stranger appeared—he stimulated them and aroused their curiosity. Perhaps the frequent cases of young people who begged may have stemmed less from poverty or greed than from a compulsion to get involved with a stranger and establish some sort of contact. What they seemed to love above everything were little games of joking make-believe, and begging provided lots of opportunities for that. Once I passed two boys sitting on a wall, and when they saw me, they begged for cigarettes. I had seen that one of them had a box full, and I said: "Why do you beg? I can see that you have lots already." They protested, "No, no"; and one of them took the cigarettes out of his pocket and handed them to the other. He knew that I saw what he had done, and he said, laughing, "I have no cigarette!" When I told him that I had seen him give them to the other boy, he answered, "Those are my father's cigarettes." All this was spoken in a sort of theatrical comic way, with much laughter and many playful gestures, all as if they were telling fairy tales and hoping that the listener would join with them in the game.

HAMBURG

Time passed rapidly in Naples. After six weeks I said goodby to Uncle Karl and Doris and took the train north to Graz. After I had settled down in my little room and started to collect myself, I gradually came to the conclusion that an epoch of my life was ending and that my years of wandering were over. I had greatly enjoyed this protracted adolescence; I had gotten to know a number of different environments and had collected a treasure of unforgettable memories. But I also realized that I could not go on forever in the same uncertain, irresponsible way. I was thirty years old, and for the first time I began to think seriously of settling into a life career. All the different jobs that I had had during the years of wandering had been just temporary expedients to provide myself with small amounts of money. I had never thought of really becoming an electrician or a teacher in an orphanage.

As I began to consider what I might do with my life, I felt more and more that free-lance writing or painting, vaguely formed ambitions of my earlier years, would not provide me with a solid foundation on which to build. My talents for creative work in those fields were too slight or too erratic and unreliable. And I remembered what my father had said earlier about keeping the arts as hobbies and not trying to live off them. I finally said goodby to what I felt had been unrealistic dreams and was grateful for my lack of will power where they were concerned. If I had had more will power, I might not have given up my ideas about writing or painting so easily. I might have strained and pushed on and found myself a feeble flame in a world that demands much more.

My interest in psychology, on the other hand, had grown stronger and more persistent over the last years. In the course of my wanderings I always had some of my notes with me, mostly notes dealing with psychological problems, and I was thinking about them and adding to them as time passed. Partly they had to do with perception and ideas that grew out of my thesis, and partly with all kinds of problems about interpersonal relations. I was also encouraged to think of making a career in psychology by the fact that after my paper ''Thing and Medium,'' to use its English title, had been published in the spring of 1926, several people had expressed their interest in it.

I began to feel sure that my ideas, though most of them were still embryonic, held promise of future development, and I was convinced that I would never get tired of psychology and that its problems would always fascinate me. Not the least factor in this decision was Lewin's continuing interest. He had been instrumental in getting my paper published, and when I was at the orphanage, he wrote me that he had treated it extensively in his seminar. He added:

"It is difficult for most people to understand, probably because it is so difficult to get the right attitude [*Einstellung*] toward the world. I have tried very hard to make it clear and to show what great fundamental progress for the whole theory of knowledge is contained in this paper."

I should mention a consideration that made me hesitate about choosing a university career, which was of course what psychology would mean. That had to do with the convictions and life style of my father. He was critical, on the whole, of university people. Already when I was in the gymnasium, I had been aware of his feeling that professors were mostly on the pompous, stodgy, pedantic side and that the picture that Goethe presents of them in the figure of Wagner in the drama *Faust* is more or less correct. An important facet of my father's character was that he became annoyed with anything that smacked of starchiness or formality. The fact that as a man of almost sixty he could enter into a happy marriage with a twenty-four-year-old girl belonging to the Youth Movement tells a great deal about him. I gradually came to realize that all his life he had mildly rebelled against social conventions and social clichés, and against any kind of routine as well. He was never extreme in these convictions, but among the two brothers and the sister with whom he grew up, he was thought of as a sort of free spirit who somehow lacked discipline.

All this endeared him to me. On the one hand, I had real respect for his feelings about the university atmosphere. On the other hand, most of the professors I had come to know were not dried-out brain machines without hearts, as he seemed to believe—quite a few of them enjoyed rich and thoroughly human lives. I gradually came to the conviction that the picture I had gotten from my father about university life in Austria and Germany, while it might be partly correct, was also a bit one-sided.

Anyway, I thought that I could risk these dangers, and I decided to look for some kind of job as a university assistant—in American terms, roughly equivalent to an assistant professorship. Since the possibilities of getting such a position were much greater in Berlin, I packed my knapsack and went there in November 1926. My uncle and Doris were still in Naples, so I rented a room in the inner city, near the Psychological Institute, which was still in the old palace. The streets in this region were usually crowded with hurrying, jostling people; so for my daily walk, I often climbed to the flat roof of the building, using the narrow stairway that I knew from my earlier visits to the institute. The air was good up there above the bustle of everyday life, and I enjoyed the quiet.

Word got around that I was looking for an academic position, and while I waited to see what might come, I again spent my time visiting lectures and seminars. I remember one of Lewin's in which he was discussing embarrassment. He asked two students, a man and a woman, to volunteer for a brief experiment. The task he gave them was to dance in front of the class. After they had danced for five or ten minutes, he asked them for self-observations, and then got the group involved in a discussion. After these seminars, most of us went to a nearby café and continued the discussion of the day. I came to know Lewin's students, among them three Russian girls—Tamara Dembo, Bluma Zeigarnik, and Maria Ovsiankina. I was soon having long discussions with them, especially with Tamara, since her interests, like mine, were directed toward emotions and personal relations. It was probably about this time that I suggested to a group of graduate students that we have regular meetings at which we would tell each other about our work and interests. At one of the first meetings I gave a talk on the observations about anger that I had collected during the dreary postwar period of 1919.

There were two developments in Lewin's work that were especially important to him at this time. One was the taking of moving pictures of children's behavior. He had made a great number of such pictures, showing small children either in free-play situations or in loosely controlled experimental situations. One of these sequences, for instance, dealt with a child's behavior when a barrier prevented him from obtaining a desired toy.

A second new development concerned the use of topological concepts in psychology. He had always been concerned with the way in which we think about psychological processes and how we represent such processes in our theories. He had learned from the philosopher Ernst Cassirer about the importance of mathematical language in the natural sciences, and he had found a kind of mathematics called topology that he believed would fit psychological problems. I remember when he first told me about his use of topology: it was a cold winter evening, and some snow had fallen. While we waited for a tram, he used the tip of his umbrella to trace a small circle enclosed by a larger oval on the snow-covered pavement. He explained that these figures represented the person within his own life space. Then he drew a little plus sign within the oval—that was the person's goal—and a line separating the person from the goal, which was a barrier. Thus he was able to represent many situations by means of topological mathematics. These symbolic diagrams were very convincing. They also provided an admirable method for thinking about different kinds of action and life situations and for discussing them with others. By offering a language more rigorous than that of everyday life, they were helpful in suggesting new theoretical formulations for study. Later in this report I will discuss the method further and will try to explain why I stopped using it, as Lewin himself did in his later work.

The early spring of 1927 was an exciting time for me. Within a period of a few weeks I received three job offers. The first was from Graz: the government of the Province of Styria planned to establish a small psychotechnical institute, and I was asked to head it. Next Karl Bühler asked me to go to Vienna as his assistant. He had been impressed by some of the ideas in my paper "Thing and Medium" and had used them in his book *The Crisis in Psychology*, in which he presented a number of different theories with suggestions as to how each could find a place within an encompassing framework. Lastly, there was an offer from William Stern in Hamburg, who was looking for someone to lecture on psychology to students of education. It seemed wonderful to have these three offers all at once and to have the possibility of choosing. But which one to take? I went to G. J. von Allesch and asked his advice. I think that I have not mentioned Allesch, with whom I had often chatted when I was in Berlin. He was at that time one of the assistants at the Psychological Institute, an Austrian and a highly cultured man who was also an art historian. When I asked him what I should do, he answered: "If you go to Graz, you will be a local celebrity because you write dreamy little fairy stories, but you will gradually fizzle out. If you go to Vienna, you will spend time in the coffeehouses and in the evenings go dancing with the beautiful girls. I advise you to go to Hamburg. You will not find many temptations there. You will settle down and do some decent work. Send me offprints whenever you publish something."

I did not see the choice quite in those terms, but I agreed with him about accepting Hamburg. True enough, in many ways it would have been very pleasant to go back to Graz. I would have enjoyed frequent visits with my father and his new young family—it would have been fun to be able to play with his two little girls more often. And there were still mountains in Styria that I had not climbed.

And how about Vienna, the city where I had been born but which I hardly knew? For a long time in my youth I would have given anything to have been able to live in Vienna. Gusti, the cousin who had helped me during the last several years, lived there. He and the two aunts would have spoiled me and smothered me with love and care and probably would have tried to supervise my life as well. They would have expected me to live with them—not to have done so would have hurt them deeply. Choosing Graz or Vienna would have meant, in a way, going back, embracing the safety and security of the familiar environment. But there was still something alive in me of the old desire to wander and get to know new places and new life situations. I had never been to Hamburg, and I had never seen the North Sea, though I had heard a great deal about the big ships that sailed from that region to America. And still more important was the fact that Stern, Cassirer, and Werner were all in Hamburg, and this would give me an opportunity to learn new aspects of psychology. So I chose Hamburg, arriving there in April 1927.

Hamburg was a big, flourishing city with a large, beautiful lake in its center. One of the first things I did after I arrived was to find out where I would go for my Sunday walks. I bought a map of the region. There were no mountains, but then, I did not expect any. However, there seemed to be lakes on all sides, and that was something.

I soon found the Psychological Institute, which at that time was located in a very old, somewhat ramshackle building in the center of the old part of the city. I was given an office high up, from which I could look out across blocks of weatherbeaten roofs. Stern welcomed me in a very nice way, and I had the feeling that he would be an altogether kind department head. As I got to know him better, I realized that he was a complicated sort of person behind a simple front. In talking to him, I always felt that there was something lacking, some kind of warm person-to-person feeling that was so strongly present when I talked, for instance, with Werner or even with Cassirer, though I knew Cassirer much less. Yet I never doubted that Stern was an imposing thinker who had somehow a vision of the whole area of psychology, beginning with some of the most basic philosophical problems and moving on to a wide range of applications in a manifold of concrete life situations. He stands as one of the founders in several fields of psychology—in child psychology, in the psychology of individual differences and testing, in legal psychology, and others. He was the first to suggest the use of the intelligence quotient. He was at once the man of practical affairs and the highly sophisticated philosopher. And he was also the very subtle observer of psychological states and processes, which has made him seem akin to the more recent existentialists or phenomenologists in some of his writings. His psychology even had a place for the troublesome problem of intentionality or representation, which was familiar to me from Meinong but which is often pushed under the rug or not perceived at all.

There was a profound difference between the views of Stern and those of the gestalt psychologists, though as far as I know they did not indulge in open polemics. The Berliners were monists. They preferred a belief in the essential equality of physical and psychical events, while Stern's philosophy was based on a profound dualism, the difference between "person" and "thing."

Comparing Stern with Meinong, I would have to concede that Stern's thinking did not show Meinong's logical precision. Comparing him with the Berlin gestalt psychologists, one feels that his theories are not as firmly anchored in experimental results or in striking demonstrations. On the other hand, I would think it quite possible that in fifty or a hundred years, psychology in general will show more similarities to Stern's basic ideas than to those of Meinong or the gestalt psychologists.

The departments of philosophy and psychology used some of the same rooms, and I often met Cassirer there when I visited his lectures and seminars. He was also an impressive person, with the eyes of a poet and a magnificent way of lecturing. His memory was phenomenal; he could quote long passages from Kant or Plato without using the text. I believe that at that time he was working on the third volume of his monumental work on the symbolic forms, in which he analyzed the schemata that are used in perception, myth, language, and science to assimilate or think about the environment. Looking back now at this time more than fifty years ago, I feel that this contact with Cassirer, slight though it was, played a part in my gradual development. It seemed to bring some of Meinong's ideas down from their monastic heights into a more human atmosphere. At the same time, it helped me to understand Lewin's theoretical position, something that was not surprising, since Lewin had taken a course with Cassirer in his student days and had written: ''Scarcely a year passes when I do not have specific reason to acknowledge the help which Cassirer's views on the nature of sciences and research offered'' (quoted by Alfred Marrow in *The Practical Theorist*).

I should mention that when I was in Hamburg, I heard that the philosopher Martin Heidegger was to give a lecture at Kiel. I decided to attend, and when Cassirer somehow learned that I was going, he asked me to give Heidegger a message. At that time I thought of Cassirer and Heidegger as the two greatest living philosophers, and I was very proud to serve as a messenger between them.

Another member of the staff was Heinz Werner. When I think of him, I always have a picture of his bemused grin and his twinkling eyes before me. He was a thoroughly humane person, with a warm sincerity that was engaging. He was a quiet man who loved his little jokes. I read his classic book on developmental psychology right away. I was especially impressed by his wonderful collection of examples of primitive thought. Later I used it as a text in seminars on child psychology. From our first meeting I felt close to him, and I enjoyed frequent visits with him in Hamburg and later in America until his death in 1964. There was also a very bright graduate student who will appear in later pages of this account, Martin Scheerer.

Of the other members of the Hamburg Institute, I want especially to mention Dr. Martha Muchow, a tall, rather heavily built woman, with a sensitive and imaginative mind, who published interesting papers based on observations of children. She was an utterly decent person, the best type of North German. She committed suicide soon after the Nazis took over the Hamburg Institute.

Altogether I feel that I was very fortunate to have been a member of the institute during this period—a sort of golden age in its history, I am sure. There was an excellent spirit in the group: the senior members seemed genuinely interested in what the younger people were doing, and we, in turn, had respect for them. Stern and Cassirer were on good terms with each other, and there seemed to be no petty jealousies or childish quarrels among the assistants.

Every so often the older students had free-for-all discussions with the assistants and some of the professors. I remember one of these occasions when Stern defended the position that science presupposes some kind of generality and that there cannot be a science of an individual object. I tried to question his claim, suggesting that there might be a science dealing with the moon, which is an individual object. I do not remember to what conclusion we came, but there was a heated discussion with much laughter.

There was also a connection with the famous biologist J. von Uexküll, another member of the Hamburg faculty, one who liked to get into debates with the psychologists. His kind of biology was very close to our interests, and it is interesting that his most important concept was that of the life environment of an animal, something that can be seen as being close to Lewin's concept of the life space.

Soon after I settled in the Hamburg position, I paid a visit to my father in Graz. Though I had been very close to him as I was growing up, I had not seen him often after I had left Graz. When we were together, we had not had time for the long philosophical discussions that we had involved ourselves in earlier, but we still had our little jokes, which his young wife shared with us. I always had a good time with their two little daughters when I saw them. I never knew quite how he felt when I entered the university world about which he had some reservations, but I am sure that he was pleased that, contrary to his expectations, I had changed from the irresponsible ne'er-do-well and become an established breadwinner with a respectable salary.

This was the second development with which I had surprised my father and all the relatives. The first, of course, was acquiring the degree. But then, once having gotten it, I had seemed to fall back again into the kind of aimless life that they thought of as typical for me. What they more or less expected at that point was that I would gradually become like some of the men of bygone generations in our family, who were said to have ended up in the country, living in happy seclusion, often surrounded by beloved pets, as they busied themselves with their hobbies.

At this visit my father was obviously happy and reassured that at last I had a job that seemed solid and well paid and that opened the way to further development. He asked many questions about Hamburg and the work that I was to do. I have often felt afterwards how fortunate it was that I was able to relieve his anxieties about me at that meeting, for he died suddenly not long afterwards. The last letter that reached me from him brought back memories of the talks we had in our old days together: he asked me whether I could explain to him what Einstein's theories were all about. The news of his death reached me when I was back in Hamburg. It meant the end of still another era in my life.

As I have said, my work was to give lectures and seminars on psychology to students who intended to become schoolteachers. It gave me good experience in speaking before a class, and somewhat to my own surprise, I soon got used to it and even rather liked it. It was, after all, an opportunity for me to talk with others about what interested me most. It also led me to think about the situation of the classroom and about the interpersonal relation between teacher and children, in which these young people in front of me would soon be engaged. I tried to locate literature that dealt with such problems in human relations. I could not find anything at that time, though there were many tomes about the philosophy of education.

Once I taught a seminar in which I asked students to write down their memories of incidents in their own early school lives that were relevant to the attitudes of children to teachers and of teachers to children. These incidents were not supposed to deal with methods of imparting knowledge but rather with the general school atmosphere and the emotional meaning of teacher-pupil interactions. This material from the students was very rich. I think it gave me more of an idea of the meaning of respect and trust, of affection and jealousy, of threat and pity, and of many other emotions and attitudes that occur in a school situation. I have never worked through all these reports, partly, I am sure, because at the time I felt rather helpless in tackling them. I realized that I lacked a network of clear concepts and a knowledge of their interrelations that would enable me to make the descriptions of concrete cases meaningful. This, of course, was the difficulty that had stumped me in my work on observations of anger ten years earlier.

Neither this attempt to treat problems of the school situation nor the earlier attempt to analyze situations concerning anger was nourished by a conscious plan to work toward a psychology of interpersonal relations. But certainly I had a vague general interest that kept pushing me in that direction. I think, however, that I was already fairly clear about the reason for my dissatisfaction with what I had done so far. I base this belief on the draft of a letter that I wrote at that time and which I still possess. Stern had told me that he had a friend who was looking for a young psychologist for a position where there was a good opportunity for promotion.

He advised me to write to this friend; he said that he would hate to lose me, but that Hamburg was still a young university where chances of promotion were poor. I started a correspondence with Stern's friend: in order to justify, somehow, the fact that I had not published any experimental papers, I explained my attitude toward experiments. I quote from this letter in which I now notice a strong influence of both Cassirer and Lewin: "Whenever I begin to think about specific experiments that I might do, I am confronted with theoretical problems whose solution does not require experiments but which can be thought through on the basis of the ordinary experience of everyday life. Only when I have cleared up the basic concepts would I feel it proper to proceed to experiments." That was my feeling at the time, or at least how I explained to myself that I had never published a regular experiment. In the end, nothing came of this correspondence.

In my not-very-systematic groping at this time toward a psychology of interpersonal relations, I also tried other approaches. At one point it struck me that names for personality traits were often related to interpersonal behavior. With this thought in mind, I tried to analyze examples of personality descriptions, but I did not get very far. Long afterwards I came to the conviction that one should not try to formulate a theory of interpersonal relations by exploring trait names; rather, one will have better results by proceeding in the opposite direction. In other words, one will get a better idea of the meaning of trait names if one already has a theory about interpersonal behavior.

During this time in Hamburg I became involved in looking at some rather unorthodox approaches to the psychology of individual differences, including graphology and astrology. I wanted to find out whether their systems of describing personality have value, regardless of the connections with the stars or handwriting that have been claimed for them. I found these systems highly interesting in themselves, but I did not see how they could help me with what I was trying to do.

I also wrote a paper entitled, in translation, "The Function of the Perceptual System." In it I carried further the thoughts that I had presented in "Thing and Medium." I tried to describe what I saw as the four main components of the causal process that is usually involved in perception: (1) In the part belonging to the environment we first find the object—for instance, the house at which we are looking. This is sometimes called the *distal stimulus.* (2) Next is the *proximal stimulus* that impinges on our eyes. (3) In the part of the process belonging to the person there are the processes in the organism that are more or less correlated to the proximal stimuli. (4) Finally, there is the experience that refers to the distant object.

When I wrote this paper, the psychology of perception did not usually try to deal with 1 or the relation between 1 and 2. I suggested that it was a mistake to omit not only this ecological phase from consideration but also the tasks that are imposed by the environment and that the organism solves in a meaningful way. I tried to show how one could treat different problems from this point of view, and I submitted that the existence of the so-called perceptual constancies is a necessary consequence of certain features of the environment.

I now have the feeling that this paper was written in a style that is not very clear, and I can believe that rather few people have read it. But I cannot refrain from mentioning that Egon Brunswik told me that the thoughts contained in it served as the basis for much of his theory. This was at the American Psychological Association meeting in Montreal in 1954; it was the last time I saw him.

All my life, wherever I have been, I have tried to get people together for discussions. In Hamburg, I suggested to Werner that I see whether Lewin would meet with the two of us somewhere between Berlin and Hamburg. Werner, who had a high opinion of Lewin, liked the idea; so I wrote to Lewin. He was also all for it, but characteristically, he thought at once of a larger gathering, including Köhler and Wertheimer and perhaps a few others. In the end he took over all the arrangements, and that is how the meeting in Rostock in the spring of 1928 came about. Wertheimer and Köhler came with Lewin from Berlin, A. Michotte from Louvain, E. Rubin from Copenhagen, Werner and I from Hamburg, with David and Rose Katz acting as our hosts in Rostock. Koffka was probably in America just at that time and so was not one of the party. They were all either gestalt psychologists or were closely associated and in sympathy with the ideas of the gestalt group. It was Rubin who first discussed in detail the importance of the distinction between figure and ground for perception. Katz had investigated the phenomenon known as color constancy. Michotte was known in later years for his study of perception of causality. Certainly this was not what I had in mind when I suggested a cozy little meeting with Werner and Lewin, but it was an interesting and friendly get-together. In the evening, Wertheimer entertained us at the piano. I enjoyed his special physiognomic game for the first time: he would play a melody, and the rest of us would try to guess which of the group his melody portrayed.

I listened eagerly to the debates that went on, but I have to confess that I remember very little about the topics that were taken up. The only item that comes back to me now is a contribution by David Katz. He told us that his two sons had different preferences in regard to food—the one liking meat; the other, vegetables. He had also noted a marked difference in their features: the one who preferred vegetables had a longish face, while the one who preferred meat had a face that was more nearly square. He wanted to find out whether this relation between food preference and shape of face was generally true; so he had perfected a method of producing a composite picture of a group of people in order to test it. To

The 1928 meeting at Rostock, Germany. *Left to right*, Fritz Heider, Kurt Lewin, David Katz, Heinz Werner, Rose Katz, Wolfgang Köhler, A. E. Michotte, E. Rubin, and Max Wertheimer

do this, he had copied photographs of perhaps ten people, one on top of the other but in such a way that the eyes fell on the same place for all ten. Then he got ten boys who preferred meat and ten who preferred vegetables from a school class. The composite pictures showed just the differences that he had anticipated. In the course of the gathering, Katz's assistant took pictures of our group and made a composite picture of us. I kept this picture for a long time, but the last time I looked for it I could not find it.

In April 1929 I went to Vienna to attend a meeting of the German Psychological Society. I will never forget the banquet in the big festival room of the Vienna City Hall. When I gave my name to an official-looking girl at the entrance, she said: "Oh, Dr. Brunswik is expecting you. I must tell him!" A moment later, there was Egon Brunswik, whom I had never met before. He was an assistant to Bühler and was one of the people in charge of the arrangements for the meeting.

He led me to a table set for four, and we had dinner with Else Frenkel, who was to become Else Frenkel-Brunswik in their American days, and Ludwig Kardos, later a professor at Budapest. Right away they began to talk about my paper "Thing and Medium," and they said how much it had interested them. They said that it implied a new view of perception—actually what Brunswik would later call the "ecological" treatment of perception. They were very much in sympathy with my approach and said that when Bühler gave his seminar on perception again, he intended to treat it from that point of view. All this was very intoxicating for me. I loved the recognition though I was slightly skeptical. I had not expected the paper to be an immediate success. In fact, I thought that it might begin to be known thirty years after its publication.

I am indebted to Bühler and his students for slight contacts with two groups in Vienna that were of great interest to me—namely, the psychoanalysts and the neo-positivists. My contact with the psychoanalysts came about when I ran into Bühler as I stopped off in Vienna on one of my trips between Hamburg and Graz. Bühler said: "Why don't you come to my house tonight? There is to be a discussion with some psychoanalysts." I accepted, of course, but I was rather surprised, because it was generally known that the Bühlers did not have a high opinion of Freud and that their students were forbidden to go into analysis. As far as I know, Else Frenkel was the only one who did, and she had to keep her visits to the analyst a secret.

When I arrived at Bühler's, there were a few analysts already there, among them Heinz Hartmann. They were sitting huddled close together on a sofa, and I had the impression that they were somewhat abashed. I imagine that they were experiencing mixed emotions. On the one hand, they could not help being impressed: a full professor at a major university like Vienna was endowed with enormous prestige; he was a prince of science who could look down on ordinary earthlings. At the same time, I am sure that they despised him and his psychology as being desiccated and academic. I cannot recall the arguments that were presented by the two sides, though I remember very well an embarrassing or slightly ridiculous incident that happened during the discussion. Bühler mentioned something that he said came from Freud's book on dreams. One of the analysts objected: he doubted that Bühler's quotation actually came from Freud. "I can show you," said Bühler, whereupon he took a volume from his bookcase. It turned out to be a new volume whose pages, after the fashion of European books of that time, had not been cut. This seemed to show that Bühler had not read the book. Of course, he explained that he had read the *Interpretation of Dreams* long before in another edition. Nevertheless, it was hard for people to suppress little snickers, and altogether the evening seemed to me rather a flop. The discussion did not reveal a common ground, nor did it succeed in exposing the differences between the two points of view. The psychoanalysts were seen by most of the psychologists as a bunch of highly imaginative and sex-ridden fabulists whose picture of the workings of the mind was never subjected to any sort of experimental test, while the psychoanalysts thought of the academics as utterly shallow and inane, representing a science that overlooks what is important, either because of plain stupidity or because they were afraid of what it might uncover.

Thanks to Else Frenkel, I also had the opportunity of attending a meeting of the Vienna circle of neopositivists. She had a high opinion of this group, and she offered to take me to one of their gatherings. She and I went into a big, dark room, which at first seemed to be entirely empty. Gradually I could see that there were some chairs standing around in an irregular fashion and that people were sitting in a few of them. After a while, someone started mumbling, and Else whispered to me that it was Otto Neurath. Eventually other people joined in, but I don't think I ever understood what they were really talking about. Except for Neurath, none of the better known members of the circle had been present, and Else agreed with me that the meeting had not been very exciting.

One thing that made my life in Hamburg very different from the life I had led before was that for the first time I did not have to worry about money. To buy a book I wanted, to go out for dinner, no longer presented a problem. My room was large enough so that I could have a rented piano in it, and I even bought a tuxedo and took in the carnival dances. Another pleasant thing about the Hamburg life was that some people whom I had known elsewhere came to visit. There was Otto, who just then was living not far from the city, actually holding a position that he heard about because it had first been offered to me and I had let him know about it. While I was still in Czechoslovakia, I had received a letter from a woman who had an experimental school for girls near Hamburg. One of the psychologists that I had known in Berlin suggested that I would be the right person for that school, and she had offered me a position as a teacher. I wrote that I could not accept her offer; I recommended Otto, who went to the school and remained for several years. It was there that he met the girl who later became his wife.

Otto visited me in the spring of 1928 after he had left the school and was on his way to Frankfurt to see Max Scheler, who at that time was a very well known philosopher. He had been influenced by Edmund Husserl, the phenomenologist, and had written on many problems from the point of view of an "understanding psychology." Otto wrote enthusiastically from Frankfurt about the stimulating and inspiring discussions that he had had with Scheler. Then Scheler died suddenly, and Otto was at a loss about what to do. In the end he went to Freiburg to get into the same kind of contact with Heidegger. Besides Otto, there were other visitors. Gerti came twice, and Doris and her father made a visit.

93

Cassirer was rector of the University of Hamburg during the academic year 1929/30. At a German university a rector is elected every year by the faculty. He represents the university at ceremonial functions but does not have much to do with the day-by-day running of the institution. As I have said, there was a close relationship between the departments of psychology and philosophy at Hamburg. So, when Cassirer became rector, the two joined forces to celebrate the occasion at one of the big dance halls in Hamburg. The assistants had prepared a number of skits as part of the festivities. I played Pavlov's dog in one of them. I remember that Cassirer said that my bark was very convincing—he even thought that he could detect a Russian accent.

The evening became important to me for a different reason. In the midst of the gathering I met Stern, who asked me whether I would like to go to America. Without a moment's hesitation I said, "Yes." He explained that Koffka, who was at Smith College in Northampton, Massachusetts, was looking for a psychologist to do research related to the education of deaf children at a school in the same city. Stern had asked Werner first, but Werner did not want to leave Hamburg. His architect wife had just finished a beautiful little house where they were now living. They could not bear to go away. Also, Werner disliked any sort of moving about or change.

When I look back now on this decision, to which I came so quickly, I cannot help thinking about the great difference between appearance and reality, between what I thought I was deciding and the real effects of this decision. I thought that I was choosing a relatively short interruption of my Hamburg life, after which I would return and go on as before. Actually, the result of my decision was a fundamental change in my whole way of living and of the possibilities for my later development. If I had stayed, I could have kept my Hamburg position, but what those next years would have meant to me and how I would have weathered them is another question.

America

Actually, the idea of coming to America was not as strange to me as one might suppose. In 1906, after the San Francisco earthquake, my father thought seriously of going there. As an architect, he was sure that he could find good opportunities for employment. I remember that we were all reading books about America, "the land of limitless possibilities," and that my father and brother and I became quite excited about the idea. In the end we gave it up because of my mother: she had grown up in Vienna, and life in Graz, only four hours away by railway, already meant an exile that she had found hard to bear.

It took only a short correspondence with Koffka, and I was appointed to the Psychological Division of the Research Department of the Clarke School for the Deaf in Northampton, Massachusetts, and as assistant professor of psychological research at Smith College. I already knew some English and was soon taking lessons with a Mormon from Idaho, who was lecturing on American literature at the university. He warned me that I should say, "Noo York," not "Nyoo York," which sounded affected to the American ear.

I also received much advice from people who had

visited the United States. An art historian, who was at that time at the Warburg Institute in Hamburg and whom I would know again in the United States during the period a few years later when so many were leaving Germany, told me that it was interesting to visit the United States but that I should not stay more than one year.

I had another long discussion with Lewin and his wife, Gerti. It was a sunny afternoon as we sat in the garden of a café in Potsdam above the river Havel. I think it was at that time that Lewin told me about a paper he had just finished and in which he had applied his topological concepts to problems of reward and punishment. It is a beautiful essay, and the fact that few people now know it is a sad example of the waste of good psychological literature. A translation by Adams and Zener was published in their 1935 volume entitled *A Dynamic Theory of Personality.*

When the day for my departure came nearer, the young people of my department arranged a farewell party for me. One of them used astrology to make fun of me in a good-natured way. Starting with the date of my birth, he described me as a typical Aquarius, and I was surprised that I fitted this type in many ways. I also received an unexpected farewell greeting from the place of my birth with a real old-world flavor. I had written to Vienna for the birth certificate that I needed to enter the United States. It was sent to me by a priest who seemed to be in charge of the office that issued such papers. He added the following note in Latin: "Finis coronet opus! Ut omne tibi bonum, faustum felix fortunatumque sit!" (May the end crown the work! May everything come out happy for you!")

On 22 August 1930, I sailed from Cuxhaven. I spent about a week in New York. I don't remember much about that week except for a general feeling of exhilaration at being at last in the fabled land about which I had read as a boy. For me, as for many Europeans at that time, the simple word "America" implied something extraordinary and stupendous. The very idea of being in America gave me the feeling of participating in an admirable adventure, in something that pointed to the future and not to the past. But I soon left New York because I was eager to get to Northampton and find out what kind of place it was.

When the train pulled into the station of the little city and when I saw the green hills that surround it, I knew right away that I would like the region. Koffka was still away on his vacation—the school opened earlier in the fall than did the college—and he had written me the address of the apartment that he had asked one of his assistants, a Miss Moore, to engage for me. It was only a short taxi ride from the station to a steep little street that at once brought back happy memories of a steep little street in Mauer, near Vienna, where my mother's parents had lived and where I had loved to spend the summers when I was a child. I took this to be a good omen, and I was prepared to enjoy Northampton, though I hardly dreamed that I would live there for the next seventeen years.

Following Koffka's instructions, I soon got into touch with the unknown Miss Moore, and she introduced me to Miss Leonard, the gentle New England lady who was then principal of the school, and to Miss Yale, the retired principal, a grand and imperious woman in her eighties, who had played an important part in the education of the deaf in the United States.

Perhaps I should begin this chapter in my life history by telling something about the educational setting into which I was arriving. There was Smith College, one of what was then a group of colleges for women in the Northeast known as the "seven sisters." The president was William Allan Neilson, a Scot, who had come to Smith College from a professorship at Harvard. He had been Charles W. Eliot's assistant in editing the set of books known as *The Harvard Classics*, which was intended to contain the essentials of a "liberal education." His numerous contributions had made

97

him an important figure in the field of English literature. Above all, he was a man of great human warmth, with a quick, puckish sense of humor, an outspoken liberal, and a firm believer in America as the country where, beyond any other he knew, each person had the opportunity to reach the level in life to which his own abilities entitled him. He left Harvard for the presidency of Smith College in 1917 with the understanding that his duties as president would always allow him time to be a teacher. As long as his health permitted, he continued to give the Shakespeare seminar for which he had been famous at Harvard. His first years at Smith College had been tumultuous. He had come soon after America's entrance into World War I. There was criticism of his German-born wife and of the German house-keeper and governess who were major figures in the president's house. His support of academic freedom for members of the faculty and his stand on some of the political issues of the postwar period called down the wrath of organizations like the Daughters of the American Revolution and the newly formed American Legion. There were demands that the trustees discipline him, but as the tenth year of his presidency approached, he stood firmly as one of the great educators of his day. A fund was raised to establish, in his honor, what was then probably unknown and is still rare in an undergraduate college, a chair for research.

The gestalt psychologist Kurt Koffka was the first occupant of this "Neilson Chair." It was during his five-year tenure that I joined his staff, principally to work in the Research Department of the Clarke School.

This school, situated on a hilltop near the college, was established a few years before the college and had a distinguished history in its own right. It was one of the first in this country to use the "oral method" exclusively, to teach deaf children to communicate by speech and lip reading instead of by hand signs and finger spelling. The advocates of this method granted that the speech of persons who did not hear their own voices or those of others could never be exactly like that of the hearing persons about them and that the visual picture of speech was fleeting and incomplete compared to one that included sound. Nevertheless, they firmly believed that speech and lip reading gave the deaf child the best means available to him of becoming a real member of his family group (usually made up of people who heard) and of the larger world in which he would need to make his way. The sign language and finger spelling were more easily mastered and understood, and they were graceful to watch. But even when they began as attempts to translate the language of the setting, they usually developed their own grammatical structure and made even the printed words of the culture a second language.

The manual method was firmly entrenched in this country when a young woman, blocked in her plan to go south to teach children of former slaves after the Civil War, was asked to teach a group of deaf children in a small town of western Massachusetts. She had heard that in some European countries deaf children were taught to speak, and with a couple of helpers, she set out to do that in her small school, working one might say on faith alone, without any knowledge of the methods that had been developed elsewhere. The school grew, and its founder and her assistant, whom I knew as the retired principal, visited European schools where deaf children were taught to speak and to read the lips. They tried to apply the methods that they observed. Later, they attended lectures in Boston by a Scottish phonetician, Alexander Melville Bell, and his son, Alexander Graham Bell. The Bells' approach to speech gave these pioneers the foundation that they felt they needed, and the younger Bell was persuaded to make visits to what, by this time, had become the Clarke School in Northampton. He worked with pupils, teaching them both speech and science, and he taught phonetics to the teaching staff. It is told that while he joined in many of the school activities, he also spent time in an attic room working on the electrical gadget that the world was to know as the telephone. Dr. Bell remained closely connected with the school for the rest of his life, serving about twenty-five years as a member of what is now called its Board of Trustees, part of that time as president of that body.

It was inevitable that these neighboring institutions, Smith College and Clarke School, should become involved in each other's activities. President Neilson was a member of the Board of Trustees of the school and was serving as its president when I came to Northampton. Just at the time of his triumphant ten-year anniversary at Smith College, Clarke School was in the midst of a campaign to increase its endowment. The campaign was headed by Nellie Oiesen, a prominent alumna of Smith College, two of whose sisters had been educated at the school. During the campaign much was made of the need for research, and it was announced that part of the money to be raised would be used to establish a research department, one division of which would deal with psychological problems related to deafness. With the plan to bring an internationally known psychologist to Smith College as the first Neilson Professor, it was hoped that this man would play a part, at least, in the Psychological Division of the projected Research Department.

As all this was under way, Miss Moore, soon to be known to me as Grace, was attending nearby Mount Holyoke College and was an occasional visitor at the Clarke School, which she had known for most of her life. Her only sister was deaf and had been educated there. Her mother, who had taken the training as a teacher, at first only with the thought of teaching her own child, had been supervising teacher at the Florida School and was nationally known among educators of the deaf. Grace graduated from college just as Koffka's appointment was being arranged at Smith College, and the plan was made, as she has put it, to place her as a "decoy duck" in his laboratory to get him interested in the school. There was a year between her graduation from Mount Holyoke and the public announcement of his appointment. Grace spent this time working on a master's degree at Smith College while she lived at the school, attending lectures and observations arranged for students who were there as "teachers-in-training" and making experiments with pupils as part of the work for her thesis.

Koffka arrived in January 1928. He and Grace got on well, especially since Grace had spent part of her senior year at Mount Holyoke in a course with Dr. Samuel P. Hayes, chairman of the Psychology Department, reading what was then available in English about gestalt psychology with special emphasis on Koffka's *Growth of the Mind*. Koffka visited the school with her, became acquainted with the principal and the retired principal, and agreed to supervise psychological research. He stipulated, however, that there must be someone more advanced than she then was to head the division on a day-to-day basis. It was a time when there were more positions than "takers" in the field of psychology in the United States; so when Koffka was unable to find a suitable person here, he brought a woman from Germany who had once been his assistant at Giessen. She left after a year for a position in Germany, and it was during the next year that I was offered the Clarke School appointment.

Grace, in the meantime, had continued to work with pupils of the school, now working under Koffka's direction. This meant that she was able to tell me a great deal about both the college and the school; and her earlier acquaintance with gestalt literature and her time with Koffka's group gave us a common base for discussing the work that was going on and for planning the next steps. As we talked, I found out that the work of Katz and Lewin had been given special attention in Koffka's seminars at Smith College; and it even turned out that she had applied for a scholarship from the American German Exchange so as to be able to work with one of the gestalt group in Germany if Koffka had not accepted the Smith College position.

Our talks soon began to deal with subjects other than the immediate scene. We talked about our past lives, about our expectations and hopes for the future, and in general about what we felt was important and worthwhile in life; and we found that we agreed in many respects. I was very happy to find myself completely at home with the personal ideas of someone who had, after all, been brought up in a completely different environment and even in a different language. It did not take us long to realize that we were in love. I was fairly familiar with different shades of this delightful feeling. However, this time it took on a new meaning—it implied total trust, a conviction of permanence and uniqueness. To get married soon seemed to us the only natural and sensible thing to do. At first we wondered whether it would be wise to begin with a trial marriage of maybe a year, but we soon gave up that idea—we knew that we were entering upon a lasting relationship.

One of the first people we told about our decision was Koffka, who was very kind and understanding and gave us good advice about possible difficulties. Grace and I soon wrote to her parents, who were understandably disturbed. How could the daughter that they had always considered eminently sensible and thoughtful have been induced to participate in such a reckless adventure as a marriage to a person she had known for a relatively short time, one from a distant country at that? Her father wrote me a letter saying, in part: "You have been in America, I believe, less than three months, and yet in so brief a time you have superseded us in the thoughts, the confidence, and the very life of this girl we have watched over, ministered to and loved with an unfailing love for these many years." Of course, this was true. I myself found it astonishing, but at the same time perfectly natural. I answered him right away and told him more of myself than had seemed easy in that first letter. After this we felt that the family was more reconciled to our plans.

I had a strong feeling that our marriage was a private affair that only concerned Grace and me and, to some degree, Grace's parents. However, the Clarke School authorities saw it in a different light, and when they got to know about our intentions, they tried in different ways to stop us. A pompous member of the Board of Trustees came to my office one day and began to talk to me as though I were a naughty little boy. There was even a suggestion that our appointments might be terminated at the end of the academic year if we persisted in our plans. All that made me angry, and at one point I threatened to resign right away. We did not realize that in reality they were quite helpless— that my resignation would have been an important defeat for them, which they had to avoid at all costs. They were still in the midst of their endowment campaign, and the establishment of a research department, which was to include our division for studying psychological aspects of deafness, was one of their talking points. Koffka, with Neilson's strong backing, was the nominal director of our laboratory, and he was on our side. He had come to know us both well, and he did not feel that our marriage would be a bad thing, in spite of the fact that the shortness of our acquaintance made it seem a little irregular to the more staid members of the community. There was a real danger that if they dismissed us or accepted our resignations, Koffka would give up his connection with research at the school. The future of the laboratory would thus be doubtful, and that, in turn, could affect the success of the endowment campaign. Where would they stand with Neilson in that case? Neilson, after all, was chairman of the Board of Trustees of the Clarke School as well as being president of Smith College. He and Koffka were also good friends.

In any case, our difficulties were somehow resolved, and the day before the Christmas vacation began at the Clarke School, we were married in New York. The date was set in this way so that the people at the school, most of whom had no idea what was happening, could get the news and recover from their surprise before all of us returned after the holidays.

There was less anxiety, of course, on the part of my relatives than of Grace's. Certainly the fact that I was a man and a few years older than Grace would have made the situation different in any case, and also the fact that neither of my own parents was living: uncles and aunts and cousins don't worry as parents do! In America the general reaction was that this could have happened only with a foreigner, a European. And from Austria the comment was that only in America would an otherwise sensible couple marry so precipitately. Gusti suggested that it was probably predestined: I had grown up in *Graz on the Mur* (the Mur being the name of the river that flowed through the city), and I was marrying someone with the name of *Grace Moore*, which in Austria was pronounced in much the same way.

After a few days in New York we traveled to St. Augustine, Florida, which had been Grace's home and where her parents lived. I was happy to get to know them and the interesting old city that Grace loved, but I have to confess that I remember very little about that first visit. There had been too many new experiences during these last months. I remember best the fleeting dip in the ocean early one morning, during which I suddenly realized how miraculously everything had turned out: here was I, married and taking a swim in the ocean off the Florida coast at Christmas time. When reality is highly improbable, it gets the flavor and physiognomy of a fairy tale: that is what my life seemed to be at the moment, a Christmas story invented by some friendly, mischievous elf who was full of improbable jokes. However, I was well satisfied with this twist of fate.

Before we left Northampton, Grace had looked for an apartment that would suit the two of us. A real-estate agent, whom she consulted ''for a friend who would be there after the holidays,'' showed her several. The one she liked happened to be the lower floor of the house in which the Koffkas had the upper floor. Grace more or less asked Koffka's approval of us as immediate neighbors, and at this point he told his wife the news of our plans. So, with their blessing, we moved into our first home when we returned from Florida. It was a spacious old house in which groups of students had lived before Smith College completed its modern dormitory system. It was located in what, in our time, was known as the "college slums," a couple of blocks from the campus.

Grace and I, along with our Clarke School affiliation, were members of Koffka's laboratory staff. Koffka was a complex and intense person. He came from a family of Berlin lawyers. His style of writing was not always easy to read—I always felt that it had a complete absence of visual or spatial thinking, with great reliance on the kind of verbal argument that lawyers love and in which they excel. He was a great Anglophile, admiring everything that reminded him of England. He had had an English nanny as a little boy, and later he had studied at Edinburgh. Whenever possible he favored the English pronunciation of a word over the American. He called his headquarters the labóratory, not the láboratory. He was a generous man who had a touching admiration, a real hero worship, for Wertheimer and Köhler, with him the cofounders of the Berlin School of Gestalt Psychology.

We attended the weekly meetings of the seminar that Koffka gave for his staff along with members of the college Psychology Department and some of their advanced students and a scattering of psychologists from nearby colleges and laboratories. The seminar was a pleasant, relaxed gathering. Koffka sat at the head of a long table, puffing on his pipe, packing and repacking the tobacco in its bowl. The discussions centered on gestalt-oriented work as well as on current publications like Tolman's 1932 *Purposive Behavior in Animals and Men*, to mention one that I remember especially. Discussions were often lively, with Koffka accepting criticism of points of view that he espoused unless it suggested that someone like Köhler had made an unfair argument. I remember one occasion when this happened: Koffka, red in the face, pounded on the table with his fist and said, "I will not allow anyone to talk like that about my friend Köhler."

Two members of the laboratory staff during the year I came to Northampton were Tamara Dembo and Genia Hanfmann. Both Tamara and Genia had grown up in Russia but had fled to Germany with their families during the upheavals that came toward the end of World War I. I had known Tamara in Berlin, where she had been one of Lewin's students, writing her dissertation about experiments that she had made on anger. Genia had studied with W. Peters in Jena. Peters was a very productive psychologist, and I can imagine that there are many interesting gems from his thinking that lie forgotten in the rubbish heap of psychological literature.

Aside from the professional stimulation of these meetings, it was through them that we came to know the members of the college's Psychology Department. Those who became lasting friends included Harold Israel, who had taken his degree at Harvard under E. G. Boring, therefore with a background going back to E. B. Titchener and through him to Wilhelm Wundt, who had been a major figure in the atomistic psychology of Germany, against which gestalt psychology had risen in protest. Another member of the group from the beginning was J. J. Gibson, with a degree from Princeton, who was to become known for his work in perception, the field in which the gestalt movement had its beginnings. During the years of the seminar, Gibson often took positions in opposition to Koffka's, but always in his own friendly fashion. In recent years he has expressed his debt to Koffka for the questions that he raised, if not always for the answers that he gave. Then there were the students who became graduate assistants and took master's degrees in the department. First, there was Elsa Siipola, who later did important work with projective techniques. She and Israel were married during our Northampton years, and after earning a doctorate at Yale, she remained at Smith until her retirement. Then there came three bright young women, a striking trio of a blonde, a brunette, and a redhead. There were bets on all sides as to which of the three would become Mrs. Gibson. It was the blonde, Eleanor Jack, known as Jackie. She commuted for a doctorate at Yale, where she became an outstanding student of Clark Hull's and, like her husband, received the American Psychological Association's Award for Distinguished Scientific Contributions. I may add that their son and one of our sons are now members of the faculty at the same university and, with their wives and children, carry on the friendship between Heiders and Gibsons that began so long ago. A few years later, Mary Henle was one of the group. She is best known for her publications about gestalt psychology, especially about the work of Köhler. These were the young people whom we knew best during our Northampton days and who did much to bring me into the current of American academic life.

The Koffkas and the Neilsons were the most important people for us during my first years in this country. In general I do not want to say much in this account about persons who are still living, but I will make a few remarks about Mrs. Elisabeth Koffka, or E.K., the name that Grace gave her and which was soon picked up by our circle of friends in Northampton. A very gifted and strong personality, she had a passionate interest in the development of ideas over the centuries. She became a greatly admired teacher of history at Smith College and later turned to the writing of poems in a very personal style.

The Koffkas were good friends of the Neilsons. The president's wife, Mrs. Elisabeth Neilson, was a delightful person, a grande dame with a warm heart. She wrote a book entitled *The House I Knew*, an enchanting description of her youth in the German province of Baden near Strasbourg. I always felt close to her because she reminded me of my mother in some ways. She worked off and on for years on a paper about Rilke's poetry and about Cassirer's treatment of symbols. Every so often I used to read some of Rilke's poems with her. I confess that I never quite understood her interpretations, but I had a feeling that in her intuitive way she may have touched on something significant.

There were a number of small discussion groups at Smith College, but all of them had only men as members. Both Mrs. Neilson and Mrs. Koffka, with their lively intellectual interests, became annoyed with this situation; so they organized a group that included both men and women. It was called the Sunday Night Club or sometimes the Ladies' and Gentlemen's Club. It usually met every three weeks during the academic year. One member would give a paper, and the ten or twelve who attended the meeting would join in discussion afterwards. Grace and I were fortunate to be part of this group, which we thoroughly enjoyed. I will mention a few of the members. There was Leland Hall, of good New England background, a bachelor whose maiden aunt made a home for him, a man of many facets. The story was told that when Neilson was hiring him for the college, he asked an advisor, "Shall I make him professor of music and have him spend his time writing, or bring him to the English Department and have him spend his time at the piano?" Neilson decided on the first alternative, and Leland, while an inspiring teacher of piano, published on a variety of subjects and practiced very little except during the months preceding the recital that he was obligated to give every two years. His books included a novel that was a Book-of-the-Month-Club selection, a travel book about his wanderings in Africa, and one called *Listeners' Music*. It is probably an indication of the period in which we lived that he was said to have been the only member of the faculty who called the president and his wife by their first names.

Then there were the Bairds. Theodore Baird was professor of English at nearby Amherst College, a genial man whom we knew as a dignified member of our group but who, we heard in later years, had been very much of a clown in his undergraduate classes. His wife, Frances, was a daughter of Titchener, one of the best known American psychologists of his day, whom Koffka had come to like and admire during a year at Cornell, though their theoretical positions were sharply divergent. Titchener was originally English but had studied with Wundt in Germany.

Jean Wilson was an American of Scottish descent who had a doctorate from an English university, probably London. She taught history at Smith College. Doris Silbert had been an instructor in music when that department suffered inner stress and Neilson appointed her chairman. He then realized that the gap in rank between her and most of the members of her department was unseemly; so he promoted her to an assistant professorship. Rank and status played a very small part in the rather ideal intellectual community of the Smith College faculty of that day.

Hans Kohn had come to Smith College in the fall of 1934—that is, during the early part of the Nazi regime. He was originally Jewish Czech, with a doctorate from Prague. He had tried living in what was to become Israel but had decided not to stay there. He was deeply Jewish in his feelings, but as a historian, he had focused on the problems created by European nationalism, and he anticipated something that he saw as still more menacing in the Middle East. One of his club papers was about his life during World War I. He had served in the Austrian army, was soon taken prisoner, and had spent the rest of the war period in Russian prison camps. His relatives were able to send him parcels of food and, more important for him, of books. He began his life as a historian there with perhaps an hour a day for exercise in an enclosed courtyard. Altogether he remembered it as a happy time. When he was asked if there was nothing that he minded, he admitted that when one of his barracks mates lay on a table screaming for a while every day, he found it distressing; but otherwise, no, it had been a pleasant life.

Antonio Borgese was a well-known Italian novelist who did not get on with Mussolini—as we heard it. He came to Smith College for a one-year appointment as Neilson Professor when Koffka's five years were up, and he remained for one or two years longer as a regular member of the faculty until he left for the University of Chicago.

As I have already told, Grace and I settled down in the apartment below the Koffkas and lived our busy, quiet lives, which soon lost any appearance of improbability and harebrained adventure. It had all become solid and permanent. I wrote to Stern to release him from his promise to hold my position for me, since I soon gave up the thought of returning to Hamburg. Grace and I were constantly together during the work hours at the Clarke School and then at home or driving out along country roads of an evening in the little car that we bought early in the new year. We never seemed to tire of each other. I remember this fact especially, because I had warned Grace that I had never been as much with another person as marriage and life in a shared apartment seemed to imply and that I might now and then feel a need to spend time on my own. But somewhat to my surprise, this did not seem to happen.

But I do remember one incident in the early thirties that might have disturbed our relationship, though actually it may have brought us closer together. It involved a visiting professor, whom we had met on different occasions and whom we had liked as an interesting and stimulating person. He suddenly fell seriously in love with Grace, and he asked whether he could come to see her and have a talk with her. We never knew whether he wanted just to have an affair with her or whether he was so deluded by his infatuation as to imagine that he could persuade her to get a divorce so that he could marry her. I decided that it would be best if I kept out of it, so I took a walk and left her to cope with him.

He was somewhat older than either of us. There was something odd about the whole situation, though we liked him too much to call it ridiculous and laugh about it. Grace tried as tactfully as she could to make him understand how impossible it was for her to enter into any sort of closer relationship with him, and in the end the three of us remained friends in the same general way that we had been before.

When I look back over my life, it seems obvious that it is made up of two halves, the first thirty-four years belonging to Europe, and the second, of more than fifty years, to America. Since the early years of one's life seem to have greater weight than the later ones, these two parts may be seen as being of about equal length when one measures them in subjective time. Every so often I have thought about the effect that this break into two parts may have had on my life. Did I experience what is now called culture shock as I moved from the first half to the second? I doubt it, since the transition was made so easy for me, first because I had right away found Grace, whose ways seemed so familiar and congenial to me, and also because so many of our acquaintances at Smith College, even from the first, had also come from Europe in recent times. And of course, with the beginning of the Hitler era, we began to meet more and more people, some old friends and others who became friends, from that same background. Then, I believe that I sympathized with many of the features of American life because of my father's democratic tendencies.

Nevertheless, it is certainly true that during my first years in the new life, I sometimes felt a certain unfamiliar lassitude and a lack of inspiration. However, I always thought that the reason was the fact that I had to use a different language from my German mother tongue and that I so often had to grope for the right words. I remember sitting in my office and trying to force myself to think up new experiments, and somehow my brain refused to work.

After a bit I decided to fill these ebb tides with something that I could work at without having to have new ideas. I needed some kind of more mechanical occupation, so I started to learn statistics, which would be useful to me when I got into more creative research. At that time, statistics was still largely unknown in Europe. As far as I knew, nobody in Berlin or Hamburg was familiar with it. I took great pleasure in working through examples in the textbooks, though I soon felt that they would not help me much in the arduous task of finding profitable theoretical ideas. Years later I was reminded of these times, when I met a psychologist who had given up a promising start in social psychology to write textbooks on statistics. I told him how much I had liked his early papers, and I asked him why he had not gone on with that kind of work. He answered, "Oh, social psychology is such a grubby subject, and statistics is so nice and clean and definite."

In any case, I gradually recovered and came out of this mental stagnation, which I can hardly call depression since in spite of it I felt happy and fortunate to be in America. And there were also occasions when I had the feeling that my past life was reaching up into my present life and touching it. Something like this happened once when I was reminiscing to Grace about some of my early experiences and told her something about Ernst and his peculiarities. I had not gotten very far when she interrupted me and said that she thought that she had met him. She did not remember the name, but a man who seemed to fit my description of Ernst had appeared in Koffka's laboratory one day and had more or less demanded Koffka's help in getting a job. Koffka, who had never heard of him before and apparently wasn't much impressed by his approach, refused to write the letter that the man wanted. He left, but he wrote Koffka an angry letter afterwards, saying something about the way one German treats another when they meet in a foreign country. This letter was somehow threatening enough in tone for one of the men in the laboratory to feel that it should be shown to someone in the president's office. No more was heard about the writer at Smith College.

I protested that it was impossible that the strange wanderer I had known in Florence could have found his way to Northampton. However, Grace was right—Koffka's visitor had been no other than Ernst. It was summer, and Koffka was away, but the assistants in the laboratory routinely helped file his correspondence. Right then, late at night, because we had been driving when this conversation took place, we went to the laboratory and looked up the letter. And as we talked about Ernst, we came upon the fact that I have mentioned, that there was still another connection between Ernst and Grace, albeit a remote one. I later found out that the man, recently deceased when I was in Florence, whose library Ernst had been employed to catalogue, was one of Grace's distant relatives by marriage. His first wife had been perhaps a second cousin of her mother's, and Grace still has a silver coffee urn that his mother or perhaps an aunt had given to Grace's grandmother. Grace had a vague memory of his name having been mentioned in newspapers and noticed by her family at the end of World War I, when he was in Paris as one of Woodrow Wilson's advisors at the time of the Versailles peace conference. He had left his first wife and their sons and had married the wealthy woman for whom Ernst had worked in Florence. Grace and I were amazed at this example of the way in which seemingly unconnected events and people can be related by complicated bonds. Today we talk of the "small world" phenomenon.

In the end, Ernst seems to have done well in America. He started a psychological journal that was widely known. I remember that Grace once wrote an article for it. Once, after he was well established in this country, he came to see us in Northampton, and we had a pleasant visit. I am sure that there was no mention of his earlier visit to Koffka and that he had no idea that we knew about it. Perhaps by that time, which was probably after Koffka's death, he had no memory of it. As far as I know, he died in the sixties.

I may mention that at some time during my first years at Smith College, I began teaching a seminar on experimental psychology in the Department of Education, which brought me into still closer contact with the college community. Seth Wakeman, a psychologist who was chairman of that department, had known Koffka during his year at Cornell before he came to Smith College and was actually the person who had suggested Koffka's name to Neilson for the professorship established in the latter's honor. He was also the person under whom Grace had worked for her master's degree before I came and who had arranged her appointment as a member of Koffka's laboratory group.

A TRIP TO EUROPE
AND THE NAZI PERIOD

In the summer of 1932 we went to Europe to give Grace and my relatives an opportunity to get acquainted with each other and to show her some of the places where I had lived. We also wanted to attend the meeting of the International Psychological Congress that was to be held in Copenhagen. We went by ship, of course, and sailed for Glasgow with E.K. as a traveling companion. After seeing something of Scotland and England, we approached Austria by train. The big house near Graz still belonged to the family, and that year an unusually large number of relatives and friends came together there, which made it easy for Grace to get to know them gradually. Gusti and his aunts came; my cousin Lilly, with her husband and four children, ranging in age from perhaps thirteen to six; my cousin Alex, who had been the special friend of my boyhood; and Mizi and the two little girls, my half sisters, who were then six and four years old. After we had been there for a time, Doris and Uncle Karl arrived.

After a month at Feistritz we moved on toward Copenhagen, with a few days in Vienna in the apartment that Gusti shared with the aunts, a few days in the apartment of Doris and Uncle Karl in Berlin, and a stop in Prague, where we saw the sights and had lunch with Gerti. Grace was amused when we went through an old castle and saw the replica of the American Liberty Bell, which this country had presented to Czechoslovakia when it became a republic. The guide pointed it out to the tourists. When one of them, obviously not an American, asked, "Is it the original?" he answered scornfully, "No, the original is cracked."

In Copenhagen it was a great pleasure to meet old friends of mine from Vienna, Berlin, and Hamburg. I was sorry to see that the tension and animosity between the Bühlers and the Berlin gestalt group had not subsided: it went so far that the young people of the Vienna group were not supposed to cross the boundaries or fraternize with the psychologists from Berlin. I stood more or less outside and had friends in both camps. An interesting evening came about when some of the young people from Vienna asked me whether I could arrange a meeting with the Berlin psychologists, including Köhler, whom they would be especially interested to meet. Grace and I set up a late-evening gathering at one of the many Copenhagen night clubs. As I remember it, O. Lauenstein and H. von Restorf from Berlin were there and Egon Brunswik, Else Frenkel, and Paul Lazarsfeld from Vienna. I have a vivid picture of how we were sitting at a table, chatting as we waited for Köhler and his wife. They came into the room, stood for a moment looking at us before they sat down, and Köhler said, "Well, did you expect me to have horns?" There followed a good conversation, and we were sure that the Bühlers never heard of this clandestine affair.

The great Russian psychologist I. P. Pavlov was also at this congress. He gave a talk, which was translated—I forget into what language. He stayed at our hotel, and every morning we went down on the elevator to the crowded café with him and his faithful companion. Another visitor, as yet comparatively unknown, was Clark Hull from Yale. He happened to share a seat with Grace on one of the bus trips that the city provided for the members of the congress. They started talking, and when Hull heard that she was one of Koffka's students, he told her that he had audited a course of Koffka's one year when they were both at the University of Wisconsin, and he added gleefully that Koffka had made a behaviorist of him.

During this summer when we were in Europe, we became increasingly aware of the Nazi movement. I remember a noisy rally one night when we had stopped over in Freiburg im Breisgau on our trip across Europe to Austria. During our stay in Feistritz there was an election in which the Nazis did not do well. We listened to the news that came in over a small radio in the quarters of the caretaker of the house, and everybody was rather silent. We realized that the caretaker's family and acquaintances were pro-Nazi and that our relatives were mostly on the other side in their sympathies. Then we were on a subway in Berlin soon after, when "extras" came out saying that Hindenburg, then president of Germany, had offered Hitler a secondary place in his cabinet and that Hitler had refused it. People were saying: "This is the end of them. They will never recover from this defeat." On the whole, though, I don't think that we paid much attention to German politics. Unfortunately, these predictions about the Nazis were wrong, and in less than a year they had taken over the government.

After the Copenhagen congress we sailed for New York from Bremerhaven and settled again in Northampton, happy about the summer's trip and still more grateful for it as the years passed. There were many people in the family group that we would never see again, and much else had changed before we returned to Europe.

I still had my Austrian passport when we made that trip. But as the situation changed, I became increasingly certain that I would never return to live in Europe, and I hastened to apply for American citizenship. The legal waiting period ended in 1938, when Austria had already been annexed to Germany. The judge who presided at the naturalization hearing took the occasion to express some of his feelings. I may have been the only man of military age in the group of applicants. When my name was called, he addressed me: "Mr. Heider, do you realize that in renouncing your native country of Austria you are also renouncing Hitler and everything for which he stands?" I had no difficulty in answering, "Yes, I certainly do, Your Honor."

To go back to 1933: at the end of January another election was held, and soon after, Hitler came to power as chancellor. As it happened, Gerti Lewin, Kurt's wife, and their small daughter were with us in Northampton just then, on their way back to Germany after spending a few months at Stanford, where Kurt had been visiting professor. Kurt followed his plan to return to Germany by way of Japan and Russia, where he had speaking engagements. However, he was one of those who saw the handwriting on the wall, and he telegraphed to us and to one or two other psychologist friends in America, probably from Moscow, to ask whether we knew of any position that was available, with the explanation in understandable code, "Gertiland now impossible." But in a letter sent from the train as he crossed Siberia, he had already written, with the future clearly in mind, "The idea of emigration is harder to bear than I had ever imagined."

The first omens seemed bad, but nobody dreamed how bad it would become. Everyone knows the history of the next years. Köhler was in some ways one of the heroes of the period. As a pure "Aryan," a professor at the major University of Berlin, and a member of the Prussian Academy, he could easily have weathered the Nazi years. At first he stayed to help his colleagues in their struggle to protect their historical "freedom to learn and to teach." Lewin wrote to me from Amsterdam in May 1933 that Köhler was "the most upright of all German professors." It is probably no exaggeration to say that he risked his life by a letter that he wrote for a newspaper. He began by praising the Nazis for some of their innovations, and then he went on to criticize them for depriving the universities of their traditional liberties. Someone sent Koffka a clipping of this letter. He was deeply disturbed. How could his admired friend Köhler have acknowledged publicly that there was anything good in what the Nazis were doing? It was only gradually that we learned that it was extraordinarily brave for anyone to have criticized the regime, even in a letter that also praised it. In the end, Köhler realized that it was a hopeless battle, and he left Germany for the United States. He was first at Swarthmore College, where he was provided with good laboratory facilities and was able to bring two of his Berlin assistants, Hans Wallach and Karl Duncker.

To mention a few of the others who were best known to us: Wertheimer was soon established at the New School for Social Research in New York, which was founded to help make places for the arrivals of those years. Lewin, whose work was already well known in this country, obtained the backing of Lawrence K. Frank of the Laura Spellman Rockefeller Foundation and the General Education Board. He was first at Cornell, then at the University of Iowa Child Welfare Research Station. After a period in Washington during the war, he was invited to his final position at the Massachusetts Institute of Technology. Werner became a professor at Clark University. William Stern, who was dismissed from Hamburg when the Nazis took over, spent his last years at Duke.

I remember that he gave a lecture at Smith College early in 1935 and that he and his wife were among the first visitors to our son, Karl, who was born in January of that year. I have a copy of the English translation of their well-known book on child psychology with a handwritten dedication, of course in German, which in English would read something like, "From a nursery of the past to a nursery of the future. In memory of our reunion in Northampton, February 11, 1935."

Egon Brunswik and Else Frenkel had come to know Edward Tolman of Berkeley when he visited in Vienna. As the Nazi threat became more definite, Egon made several trips to this country, usually spending part of his time in Berkeley. He soon accepted a position there, and in 1938 Else came. Egon met her in New York, where they were married, visiting us in Northampton soon after. Lazarsfeld, who joined the faculty of one of the universities near New York, was another visitor to Northampton.

After the end of Koffka's five-year appointment as Neilson Professor at Smith College, he became a regular member of the Psychology Department and remained teaching, writing his book *Principles of Gestalt Psychology*, and continuing his experimental work with an assistant and a laboratory that the college provided. During the next years, when Köhler and Wertheimer came to visit the Koffkas, we were often invited to join their gatherings. We watched with great interest and pleasure the interaction between Koffka and the guest of the occasion. In spite of the agreement on principles that made the collaboration of this brilliant trio so fruitful, there were also differences, which meant that each had made his own contribution to their joint product. Wertheimer was the temperamental and inspired artist; Köhler was a somewhat reserved physicist, thinking very much in spatial terms; and Koffka was the highly verbal lawyer and logician, who tried to bring everything into a total system. We had the impression that Köhler's and

Wertheimer's admiration for Koffka was not so great as his for them. Nevertheless, Koffka's 1935 book, difficult though it is to read, will probably stand as a major contribution of this gifted group.

The Neilsons were very much involved with the situation in Germany. They brought Paul Nathan, who, like his father before him, had been physician to Mrs. Neilson's family, and they welcomed others to the faculty and to the college community. Paul established a practice in the nearby city of Holyoke, and he watched over many of us in an informal professional capacity. He and his mother, who joined him after he was settled, were almost uncle and grandmother to our children during the Northampton years. They were usually with us for Thanksgiving and Christmas, and the first spring after we moved to Kansas, Paul came and made a vacation trip with me to Colorado. Years later, one of Karl's sons was named Paul for him.

Koffka, as a liberal and a firm Anglophile from his youth, followed each step as the tragic drama unfolded, becoming increasingly concerned as the war began in Europe in the summer of 1939. It seemed ironic that he died the day before Pearl Harbor, which was soon followed by America's entrance into the war.

For ourselves, my Austrian background caused us little discomfort in the community, even after the United States entered the war. For one thing, we were very much sheltered by the attitude of the college; and the fact that there were so many people of Germanic background who had come as refugees meant that not everyone with a German accent was suspect, as I have heard was the case in 1917/18. I was accepted without question as an air-raid warden who patrolled the neighborhood to be sure that windows were properly covered during practice blackouts.

Nevertheless, we did not feel that our children should learn German at home during those years when we might otherwise have begun it. To have had a German-language home might have been too much even for a fairly tolerant community. And when our eldest son, then in the third grade, reported that his class was in charge of the school paper that week and that he had contributed a piece about his cousin who was a prisoner of war in Canada, we wondered whether this was wise. In the end, Grace and his teacher, who had also wondered, decided to let his item be among those that did not get into print. Of course, there was not space for everything that the children offered. Now that he is an adult, he does not remember having been frustrated when nothing came of his first attempt at publication, and I do not remember what may have been said at the time. This cousin was not a close relation—I had never met him. He had been an aviator, shot down during an air raid over England. He wrote to ask for tools and seeds for his "victory garden." We sent them, but we never learned for whose victory he wanted to plant the garden.

Along in October of 1933, the year that Lewin was at Cornell without his family, he wrote me, "What would you think of the following plan: To invite a group of younger psychologists who are actively interested in our things to get together for some discussions?" It was during the Christmas holidays of that year that the first meeting of what became loosely known as the Topological Psychologists was held. A small group met in Northampton, with Koffka's laboratory as their headquarters. Among them were Donald Adams and Karl Zener from Duke, who had spent time with Lewin in Berlin; Tamara Dembo and Genia Hanfmann; Don McKinnon; Koffka, of course; and several members of the Smith College Department of Psychology. These meetings were held every year after this except when America was in the war, always just before the meeting of the American Psychological Association. They continued for a long time, even after Lewin's death. They became larger and larger, often including a variety of people who were entirely outside the immediate Lewin group and who were brought in under

Frank's auspices to create interesting exchanges with members of the core group. I remember especially the year when Tolman came to debate with Koffka and Köhler, and another meeting when Margaret Mead and Gregory Bateson were invited. Lewin, from the beginning of his life in this country, had attracted graduate students and postdoctoral fellows who became leaders in American psychology in the years that followed. This combination of stimulating people and Lewin's geniality made the gatherings interesting and cheerful affairs, and Grace and I came to know many of the outstanding American psychologists as we attended them year after year as often as we could until the final meeting in the sixties.

Sometime during our Northampton years the Cambridge philosopher G. E. Moore, who was admired by the Bloomsbury group, spent a semester as visiting professor at Smith College. I attended his seminar a few times, but I chiefly remember his saying that one should not say, "I see a chair," but rather, "I see the surface of a chair." This annoyed me because it seemed to me to be the kind of sophistic quibbling which illegitimately disregards the well-founded assumptions about our environment on which our daily life is based. To hold this attitude consistently, one would have to say that nobody can see any three-dimensional object. I decided, probably prematurely, that I could not learn anything from such chicanery, and therefore I stopped attending the seminar. I suppose that Moore's speculations reminded me too much of some of my rebellion against Meinong when I was a student, though if I remember rightly, Meinong never violated common sense to that extent. My reaction to Moore may have been stronger because I knew that he had written at least one essay on Meinong. As I look back, I am sorry that I did not stay with the seminar and present my objections to what Moore was saying instead of acting as if I had been personally insulted. There was certainly more substance beneath this apparent nonsense than I gave myself time to find out.

While he was still in Europe, Lewin had been working on a book that was to be called *Principles of Topological Psychology*, writing it in German, of course. Grace and I offered to translate it into English, and we worked on it through the summer of 1934 when we boarded on a farm in southern Vermont. It was rather fun doing it: we would read a sentence in the German manuscript together. Then the first one who thought of an English version would say it aloud, and it would be "tossed" back and forth until we were fairly well satisfied. Then it would be typed out. We finished a first draft that summer while Lewin was in Germany preparing to move his family to Ithaca. Our first son, Karl, was born in January 1935. Lewin made several trips that allowed him to stop in Northampton through that academic year, when we worked together on phrases that we found too difficult, often persuading him to make a long German sentence into two or more shorter ones that were easier to put into English. Incidentally, a few years after Lewin's death, when a German press wanted to publish the book, only part of the original could be found. Therefore the German edition is a retranslation of our English version.

We finally thought of a plan to finish the book to our satisfaction by spending the summer together. We advertised and found a farm family near Cooperstown, New York, that would take as boarders the Lewins and their children, of four and two, and us, with our son who became six months old during the summer. We put up a tent out of doors to use as headquarters, and with our child in a "kiddy coop" nearby, we spent many hours working with Lewin to improve the translation. During the course of that summer, a young New York graduate student, who was working on a dissertation problem related to Lewin's work, came to consult with him. This was Alfred Marrow, a man who owned factories in the South and who was partly responsible, at least, for getting Lewin involved in the "action research" that later was the focus of his activities at the Massachusetts Institute of Technology.

In 1969, Marrow published a book appropriately entitled *The Practical Theorist: Life and Work of Kurt Lewin*, which was largely based on interviews with people who had known Lewin.

The Lewins were busy with their children as well, and they often stayed up late into the night writing to relatives and friends in Germany. Many Jews loved Germany and still could not believe that anything would really happen to them. They were convinced that after a flurry of unpleasantness at the beginning of the Nazi takeover, things would settle down again, and life would go on as before, with perhaps a few minor changes. Lewin saw the situation as much more threatening; therefore, he was trying to get as many as possible to leave while there was still time. He complained bitterly that many misjudged the situation completely and resisted his attempts to save them.

My Austrian relatives were not all of the same opinion about the Nazis. Uncle Karl and Doris detested them and were unhappy as they heard about the changes that were being introduced into the German universities. Mizi, my father's young widow, as a former member of the Youth Movement, had high hopes that all these upheavals would eventually lead to a good end; therefore, she was enthusiastic when Austria became "part of the Reich" in 1938. Uncle Karl died in the summer of 1935 and thus did not live to see the annexation of Austria and what came after; and Doris died in 1938, before the beginning of the war. She had had an operation for cancer the year before but felt well enough during the summer of 1938 to set out with her close friend, the author and journalist Margaret Boveri, for a trip by car to the Near East. They went by way of Istanbul and Ankara. When they reached Beirut, Doris collapsed, and the doctor whom she saw there said that she could not go on. She went back to Feistritz by train, and Margaret finished the trip, which took her to Iraq and Iran. She described it in a book entitled *Ein Auto, Wüsten, blaue Perlen* (A car, deserts, blue pearls), in which she also tells how Doris helped her cheerfully and resourcefully through many adventures.

Doris remained up to the end the courageous and adventurous person I remember. She had to undergo still more surgery. Gusti stayed with her all through it and sent me a long description of her illness and death. He told me how some of her last days were spent in burning letters, and I am sure that among them must have been the voluminous ones that I had written her during my earlier years. She had told me that she treasured them. I have often wished that I could have asked her to send them to me, but I could not have done so without admitting that I thought she was fatally ill, and Gusti had told me that she herself never talked as though she realized it. But the fact that I did not ask her for them may have given her the feeling that I no longer wanted to think about those days and the part that she had played in my life at that time.

Perhaps I should mention here something else that I regret in a similar way. I think that I have not mentioned my mother's sister, whom we called Tante Mizi. She had had polio as a child and walked with a limp. She was a violinist, and she visited us every few years when she gave a concert in Graz. She also composed and had ambitious dreams in that field. Once she began to set the *Odyssey* to music, and another time she was planning an opera about Antinous, the beautiful boy of antiquity. My father had his doubts about all this. He would slyly make fun of her in a good-natured way. When she explained one of her projects, he would exclaim ''another ice factory'' or ''another porcelain factory.'' Actually there had been members of our family who had ventured to manufacture ice and some who worked with porcelains. Both attempts had ended in failure, though the porcelain factory had a certain literary history, one might say. It was in Bohemia, near Marienbad. During its more flourishing years, Goethe once visited it. He was interested in geology and in the rare kinds of earth that are used in making porcelain.

In any case, my father had a somewhat negative opinion of Tante Mizi, whose ambitions so greatly surpassed her abilities, and I am sure that I was influenced by his feelings. For a long time I had no contact with her at all, and now that I look back, I have to confess that I never thought of visiting her when I stopped off in Vienna. Then, at the end of World War II, I suddenly heard from her. She wrote that she had a collection of letters from my mother—the sisters had written to each other about twice a week during the years when my mother lived in Graz and Tante Mizi lived in Vienna. She was eager to hear from me about my life and my family in America. She said that whenever I wrote her, she would send me a few of my mother's letters with their detailed accounts of our life in Graz and the adventures of my brother and myself. My mother had been a gifted letter writer, and it pains me now to think that I let that opportunity to acquire this treasure trove of old letters pass by. I am still baffled about my failure to take Tante Mizi up on her offer and get those letters from my mother. I can only believe that it was part of the uncomfortable state of mind into which I had fallen just at that time, but this comes later in my story.

WORK WITH THE DEAF AND WORLD WAR II

All this time, our work was continuing at Clarke School. Though I spent some time studying statistics during my first months, I did not entirely neglect my job, which was to make investigations into psychological aspects of the education of the deaf. Koffka remained director of our research; but once Grace had completed the studies that he had suggested before I came, he left us very much to follow our own inclinations, standing ready for consultation when we felt the need for advice. Over the next years we worked on a series of problems, and we wrote papers that appeared as *Psychological Monographs* in 1940 and 1941. But before I describe these publications, I would like to tell something of my more general impressions as a newcomer to a school for the deaf. I still have notes that I made after my first observations, and I am struck by how they relate to my old ideas about "Thing and Medium" in what they say about the role of language and the relations of means to ends. The growing child who can hear uses language principally to get into contact with other people and to interact with them in different ways. The better it fulfills the role of mediation, the more a person is free to concern himself with the message that is being sent and the less with the way in which it is being transmitted. But in teaching a deaf child to speak, it is probably necessary to begin by making the articulation of words the focus of attention. It is true that the teachers were very much aware of this problem, though they did not express it in my more general terms. For example, before a new word for an object or an idea was taught to a class, there was drill on the pronunciation as such, so that when the meaning was introduced, the mechanics of speaking it would come easily. Nevertheless, a child who was eager to say something was constantly being interrupted to have his pronunciation corrected. To what extent this emphasis caused meaning to recede into the background and to what extent this is unavoidable during the early years I do not know now, and I certainly did not know then. But the obvious delight with which a child in one of those small, carefully taught classes seized on each new meaning as it was given to him speaks against the immediate feeling that these corrections distract him irreparably from the content. The teacher of the beginning class told about how each year the day came when one child, and then the whole class, seemed to realize that all the objects about them had names. The children would rush around the room, pointing to one object after another and waiting for the teacher to pronounce the name each time. There was excitement in the air, as though they realized that they were building up a new medium which they could then put to use. I remembered the seminar in which Cassirer discussed this sudden realization as Helen Keller described it in her account of her early years. In any case, the more subtle and complicated questions concerning the acquisition of language tied the experiences of my new life in with my thinking of the preceding years.

Another aspect of life in the school that struck me during my first weeks was the very strict order that was maintained in the classrooms, although certainly by warm and friendly teachers. Each successful effort by a child was rewarded with immediate praise, and each child was made to feel himself a person of importance in the group; yet there was perfect order in everything that they did. It seemed too good to be true. As I watched them on the playground with a supervisory figure in the background, I knew that the shouts and squeals of laughter were very much those of an ordinary grade school, but I became curious about what they would do if they were left to themselves in a schoolroom situation.

We had had a window constructed, with a one-way screen between my office and the adjoining room, which we were to use for our work with the children. Using this arrangement, we once tried a short experiment. We asked one of the teachers to bring her class to the observation room: she was to carry on regular school work for about ten minutes, then leave the children alone. After she had disappeared, the children at first just waited, then they gradually left their seats, walked on tiptoe, and looked around, somewhat bewildered. But very soon they seemed to explode. They threw things around and pulled window shades down and tore them to pieces. When they began to break up the furniture, we asked their teacher, who was watching through the window with us, to take charge. The supervising teacher of the department that handled the younger children, who was also with us, was shocked at the scene of destruction. I hurried to the principal of the school and assured her that I had learned something from this experiment but that she need not fear that I would repeat it. Though I did not tell her so, I had certainly not expected their obedient little angels to turn into ravaging devils as they had seemed to do. One might wonder whether their behavior was proof of inborn "sinfulness," which was usually suppressed by everyday school discipline, or whether the suppression itself created the tension that was bottled up through school hours and sought release whenever there was an opportunity.

But there were other aspects of the situation: for one thing, these children lived in a boarding school. Boarding schools are necessary for many deaf children just because they need specialized instruction, and in a smaller or average-sized community, there are not enough deaf children to justify hiring a highly trained teacher for them. And however kindly the discipline of the school, the child who lives a group life twenty-four hours a day is more restricted in many ways than most children who are part of an ordinary family group after school hours. Looking back, we remember from a few years later how our own children would break loose when they came home after three hours in what seemed to be a relaxed and comfortable nursery school.

One of the studies that was to be part of the two monographs that we published from Clarke School had to do with lip reading. It was obvious that learning to read the lips involved something more than ordinary school learning. Some children who were very good at other tasks appeared to be poor lip readers, and others who did not stand out in schoolwork were excellent lip readers. We made a moving-picture test of lip reading with the help of one of the teachers who spoke the material that we and the staff had decided on for its content. Results of this test showed good agreement with the teachers' estimates of lip-reading ability in everyday situations, but it showed low correlations with results of intelligence tests and, at the same time, high correlations with ratings by the teacher of physical education on ability to follow a rhythm as shown by skill in dancing. As we looked further into this problem, it became clear that lip reading required rather special abilities that are also akin to factors that make for easy empathy with other people rather than to a more analytic kind of intellectual ability.

Among other studies that we made during these years there were several related to my continuing interest in interpersonal relations. I did not realize when I began work with the deaf how closely one of the principal aspects of deafness tied in with this interest. Indeed, one can say that deafness, because it affects means of communication, is eminently a social handicap in comparison to blindness, which is much more directly a handicap in relation to physical space. One of our studies was an attempt to describe the social behavior of young deaf children, who, in spite of the fact that they might have learned only two or three spoken words and no formal signs, interacted constantly with each other by means of facial expression and a few simple gestures. The material of this study consisted of observations of free play in groups of deaf children and in groups of hearing children between the ages of three and five years. We wanted to find out more about the actual limitations imposed by deafness—what went on among hearing children that did not occur among the deaf. I feel that the attempt to describe these differences in more general terms was helpful in my later attempts to understand more about interpersonal relations.

Another study dealt with the adjustment of the adult deaf. It was based on letters written by graduates and former pupils of five different schools for the deaf in answer to an informal questionnaire. The questions were framed to elicit the attitudes of the deaf about their own life situations: for example, When did they first realize that they were deaf and that other people had abilities that they lacked? When they were children, what kinds of difficulties did they have with their playmates who could hear? What special problems had they met in their lives after they had left school? What did they feel that they had most missed because of their deafness?

We had replies from eighty-six deaf adults, approximately evenly divided between men and women. Some of this group mentioned the absence of sound for its own sake, usually the inability to hear music, from which people who could hear so obviously got enjoyment. One remembered the period of her life before she became deaf, when she had loved the sounds of nature—the hums of insects, the croaks of frogs, the falling of rain. But it was mostly the social aspects of deafness that were mentioned, often the feeling of being left out in a group of hearing people when the conversation moves from one speaker to another in a way that even the best lip reader cannot follow unless some hearing person takes the trouble to give him the cues. Especially interesting was the attribution of responsibility for the problems that were described: in some cases the emphasis was on resentment of persons who could hear for not being more helpful, in others it was much more on the actual limitations imposed by the inability to hear and on the writer's need to deal with his life situation in terms of what he could and could not do.

In discussing employment after they had left school, some suggested that because tasks like answering the telephone in an office were clearly impossible for them, it was up to them to do other things better. And while many spoke of feelings of inferiority and handicap, others mentioned the careful training that they had received in a school for the deaf, with its small classes and individual attention, as having given them certain advantages over their hearing contemporaries.

The results of these studies and others that we made were reported from time to time at meetings of educators of the deaf, and short reports were published in the *Volta Review,* the journal that Alexander Graham Bell had established for what was then known as the American Association to Promote the Teaching of Speech to the Deaf. The 1940 and 1941 monographs contained full reports of our psychological work, a paper summarizing the year's work of my predecessor, Dr. Margarete Eberhardt, and one by Jean Sykes, later Jean Sykes LeCompte, who worked with us when she was a graduate student at Smith College.

My duties at Clarke School and at Smith College left me some time to work after hours at home on other psychological problems that interested me. In 1939 I published an article on "Environmental Determinants of Psychological Theories," which deals with a number of theories in terms of differences in the ways in which they organize their data. The distinctions between proximal stimuli and the distant environment play an important role in specifying these differences. It is evident that this paper grew out of the one on "Thing and Medium" that I had published more than ten years earlier. I now realize that it also deals with the role of attribution in psychological theories and that it approaches a whole cluster of problems that are connected with the relation of attribution to theory-building in general.

The response to "Thing and Medium" was still very limited, though a few people such as Carnap, Reichenbach, Bühler, Lewin, and Brunswik had been very positive about it and had encouraged me to continue working on these ideas. This was especially true of Brunswik, who later, in his own way, developed concepts that I had sketched in that first paper. He and I remained good friends up to the time of his early death, but I did not always agree with the direction he took in his later writing. I had the feeling that he got somehow stuck in the early views of the "Vienna Circle" of philosophers which some of its members—for instance, Carnap and Feigl—had given up as being too simple.

On one occasion I spoke with a physicist at Smith College and tried to explain my ideas about *thing* and *medium* to him, but he did not seem to understand at all what I meant. At that time, Information Theory, which nowadays makes physicists familiar with such thoughts, had not yet been born. I also gave a talk to a group of psychologists there without getting any real response.

But to go back to the more personal side of our lives: during the summer of 1935, when we and the Lewins boarded with a farm family in New York State, we looked back a little nostalgically to the summer before, when we had stayed in the hillier region of southern Vermont, which was also closer to home. During the spring of 1936 we made a couple of weekend trips to Newfane, near the region we had enjoyed earlier. We stayed at a little inn and were taken around by real-estate agents to look at property that was for sale. We finally bought a little house on a hillside in South Wardsboro. It was more than a hundred years old, dirty and in poor repair, with sixty acres, partly meadow but mostly woods and thickets. There was a deep spring just above the house, from which water flowed to a tank in our cellar and then was pumped by hand to fill another tank in the attic that supplied our relatively modern bathroom. Water for use in the kitchen was pumped directly to the kitchen sink. We had the house cleaned, and carpenters made basic repairs while we boarded with the farm family whose house was just below ours on the hill. We finally moved, triumphantly, into this the first house of which we were the actual owners. Our first night was a disaster. We soon realized that the house was alive with bedbugs. Fortunately, the small room in which Karl, by that time a year-and-a-half old, slept had been in especially bad shape and had had to be newly constructed, so he suffered no bites. We moved back into the house of the kindly farmers until we could get exterminators. The nearest ones came over a Sunday from Hartford, Connecticut, and once more we began life in our little house. Fortunately, we had a contract from the exterminators guaranteeing their work. In two or three weeks a new generation of bedbugs had hatched from eggs that were apparently immune to the fumes that had been used, and the treatment had to be repeated in another Sunday visit. After that, all went well; but our bank account was exhausted, and we had to borrow to get through until our pay checks started coming with the beginning of the new school year.

I soon decided that our woods were a little too primitive for my taste; therefore, I worked to make a path through this jungle so that I could follow a little brook down the hillside. I even started work on what we had hoped would provide us with a swimming pool, but that attempt did not succeed—the water supply was not sufficient. In the meantime we set up the tent from the summer before to give Grace and me a work place, and it was during that summer that we translated my old paper into the English "Thing and Medium." Those were the days when we had bright and attractive young girls to help with children and general housework, something that was necessary during the school term if Grace was to continue with what was really part-time work at the Clarke School after we had even one child, and in due time there were three.

A short way down one hill and up another we found summer neighbors whom we enjoyed, two philosophers from New York, Ernest Nagel and Sidney Hook and their wives. The Hooks had children who overlapped ours in age, and we became close friends and have met in different places over the years. One summer, Gerti Lewin and the two Lewin children lived in the village while Kurt made a trip to Israel. Another year, Hans Wallach and Karl Duncker, with their two mothers, spent time in the neighborhood.

There was also a chance acquaintance that we made during one of our house-hunting expeditions whom I may mention, though we settled in different villages and did not see much of each other. It was another of those "small world" incidents that happen every so often. While we were staying at the little inn at Newfane, I noticed a couple, considerably older than we, who also ate their meals in the dining room of the inn and also seemed to be going about with real-estate agents. I felt certain, somehow, from their gestures as they talked to each other, that they were Viennese. We decided to try to find out by passing close to their table to see whether they were speaking German, but we heard only a steady flow of English. I was still sure, however, that my guess was correct, and we finally spoke to them in the lobby of the inn. We learned that he was a physician, then with the Rockefeller Institute in New York, originally from Vienna. When he heard my last name, he recognized it as that of a medical-school classmate, my Uncle Adolf. His name, Karl Landsteiner, meant nothing to me at the moment; but when we mentioned it to our physician friend Paul Nathan, we learned that he was no other than the man who had been awarded a Nobel Prize for the discovery of blood groups, the discovery that made transfusions safe. The next summer I met the couple again when I was shopping at a Brattleboro market, and we exchanged a few visits.

The lasting acquisition that I carried home from the Vermont farm and of which I still have daily reminders is a strained back. This is how it came about. The front door of our old farmhouse was on one side, but the stone slabs that must have served as the steps leading up to it were lying on the ground below it, in an irregular heap. I set out to make the door usable by rebuilding the steps. I began with the largest slab, which appeared to have been used as a foundation for the others. I tried to move it, but it would not budge. I exerted all my available will power and strained to the utmost. Suddenly, something snapped, and I lay there among the slabs with an excruciating pain in my back. Every attempt to get up or to make even the slightest movement made the pain unbearable. Eventually, with Grace's help, I crawled into my bed. She called a doctor. The complaint seemed to be something with which he was familiar, but he was not able to do much to improve my condition. Gradually I was able to move about more, but I got a neighboring workman to rebuild the steps.

There is an Austrian expression for such an ailment—it is called a *Hexenschuss* (a shot by a witch)—and this seemed to me exactly what I had experienced. The collapse of a fairly strong, well-functioning body into a helpless mass of agonizing spasms was so sudden that it seemed quite plausible to explain it as the result of a well-aimed shot delivered by an exceedingly unkind, invisible power. However, sober reflection led me to the inevitable conclusion that I myself had brought about my unfortunate state. Was it not my own arrogance that had led me to think that I could lift the biggest stone just by exerting will power? On the other hand, should there not have been an internal safety valve that would automatically shut off the will power as soon as it attempted to force an action that was patently beyond the capacity of the executive mechanism? It would certainly have been better for me if my back had been able to disobey and say, ''I am not going to hurt myself trying to follow such outrageous commands!''

Of course, I soon gave up trying to fix the blame and turned toward the more practical task of getting used to restrictions of my space possibilities, to speak in Lewinian terms. There followed a period of learning to adjust to life with an injured back. Simple tasks such as picking up something from the floor or putting on my socks had to be done in a special way if I wanted to avoid a new attack of muscle spasms in my back. Heavier tasks, such as lifting and carrying and shoveling snow, were no longer for me; but every so often, when my back was feeling more or less ''normal,'' I would try again to ''do my share'' and would again meet with trouble. Two professional women were of great help to me during the years that followed this first catastrophe. One was a New York physician, recommended to me during a semester we spent at Cornell. She was Dr.

Janet Travell, whose name later became well known when she became the White House physician who had special responsibility for John Kennedy's back problem. She was a kindly, motherly woman. She made all the necessary examinations to locate the source of my repeated attacks. In the end she explained to me that scar tissue, remaining from the original accident, was responsible for what happened when I attempted anything that strained the muscles of my back. This was something that would not get better with time. I had to live so as to guard against attacks. This advice was helpful: I no longer felt that as soon as my back stopped hurting, I should try again the tasks that I had done without thought before.

The other woman who helped with my troublesome back was Fru Ness, a teacher of gymnastics in Oslo, who was suggested to me when we were spending the year 1960/61 in Norway, I with a Fulbright fellowship and Grace with a research fellowship from the National Institute of Mental Health in Washington. Fru Ness taught me a series of exercises that I have used ever since to help keep the muscles in shape and allow a little more freedom of movement. She was a sister of the well-known Norwegian philosopher Arne Ness, who had been a visiting professor at Berkeley and of whom I had heard Brunswik speak. These steps in learning to live with my injured back were a matter of almost twenty-five years.

To return to my chronological account, we had bought the farm in the spring of 1936, when Karl was a little over a year old. By our second summer there we had another son, John. After another couple of years the boys were enjoying the more primitive outdoor summers, and the tent continued to be a good retreat for purposes of work. Nevertheless, we began to realize that there was one major drawback to our location. Swimming had always been an important part of our summer life. It gradually became clear, however, that our hopes of constructing a swimming place of our own,

even with extra manpower, were doomed to failure because the water supply was not sufficient. So we found ourselves driving ten or more miles for a daily swim. Then, in 1940, Grace's mother was ill, and we spent the summer in St. Augustine within a few miles of a good beach. A third son, Stephan, had arrived by that time. World War II was under way in Europe, and it seemed inevitable that the United States would become involved. Everything felt unsettled, and in addition, we were finding two homes rather more than we could afford. We decided to give up the farm and to do more wandering during the summers while it was still possible. The farm sold quickly, and an amusing aspect of the sale was that it was bought more or less as an air-raid shelter by people who were in some way connected with the American wife of my cousin Stephan, another "small world" event.

For the next years we stayed mostly in Northampton, largely because there was gas rationing after America entered the war at the end of 1941. One pleasant event during that period was a visit to the institute of Adelbert Ames in Hanover, New Hampshire. Ames had started out as an artist, but very early he became interested in the psychology of visual perception. He discovered a defect in vision, which he called *aniseikonia*, that involves an anatomical inequality in the two retinas and produces strange visual illusions. I believe that he suffered from this problem himself and that he had discovered a way to correct it by special eye glasses. As it happened, one of the Rockefellers had aniseikonia, and

On facing page, meeting of Topological Group, 1940 at Smith College. (1) Margaret Mead, (2) J. J. Gibson, (3) Gregory Bateson, (4) Kurt Lewin, (5) M. A. Rickers-Ovsiankina, (6) Mary Henle, (7) Henry Murray, (8) Kurt Koffka, (9) Beatrice Wright, (10) Erik Wright, (11) Robert C. Challman, (12) Karl Zener, (13) Stuart Stoke, (14) Eugenia Hanfmann, (15) Jacob S. Kounin, (16) Lawrence K. Frank, (17) Erik Erikson, (18) Tamara Dembo, (19) Alfred Baldwin, (20) Ronald O. Lippitt, (21) Ralph K. White, (22) Fritz Heider, (23) Gertrude Lewin, (24) Rosalind Gould, (25) Seth Wakeman, (26) Harold Israel, (27) John Gardner, (28) Elsa Siipola

Ames had been able to help him. The Rockefellers then provided money to establish an eye clinic in Hanover, near Dartmouth College. This clinic included a laboratory where Ames could continue his experiments in vision.

But all this time, while Ames was involved in work in visual perception, he had had no contacts with professional hologists. When there was a meeting of the American Psychological Association at Dartmouth in 1936, Ames was hopeful that he could get some of the bigwigs interested in his work. He invited some of them to his laboratory; but when he showed them his demonstrations, they only shook their heads and said: "Very amusing, but we are sorry. What you have there are optical illusions that have been well known to psychology for a long time. All these problems were solved thirty years ago." They did not realize that Ames's demonstrations brought in a factor that had rarely been taken into account in the old experiments—namely, the relations to distant objects beyond the proximal stimuli, in other words "ecology."

But in spite of this rebuff by official psychology, the people who believed in the value of Ames's attempts did not give in. They found a man to join Ames's staff who could help bring him into touch with other persons working in the field of visual perception and who could translate Ames's ideas into a language that could more easily be understood in a wider circle. This man was Paul Grabbe, who invited Lewin to visit Ames's laboratory, and Lewin asked me to go with him. That is how it came about that the Lewins and we spent some time in Hanover during the summer of 1945, combining a vacation with a visit to Ames. The Lewins' children were in a summer camp near Boston, where they had been accustomed to go in the summer, and our three spent a month fairly near Hanover, where there were other children from Northampton.

At that time I was fond of a little demonstration that I had made which showed that one can produce the experience of a three-dimensional cube by means of a two-dimensional drawing seen from a particular angle. I do not mean just a drawing of a cube, but a setup that gives the experience of having a real cube in front of one's eyes. Obviously the trick consists in producing proximal stimuli which the distant stimulus would ordinarily cause, and these stimuli can often be produced without having the object present. I showed Ames one of these demonstrations, and I explained how he could build different setups that would all give the impression of three-dimensional cubes although they would actually be different wire models that would have no similarity to cubes except when each was seen from a specific angle. Ames was greatly pleased with this suggestion. When I visited him again in the fall, he had constructed a very nice setup to demonstrate the effect that I described, but with one difference that he had introduced: he used a chair instead of a cube for the model of the object that would appear at a distance. Actually this change was significant with regard to the difference between us in our ideas about perception. It was important for him to use the chair, because it had a familiar practical significance and because one could relate to it by actions—for example, by sitting in it.

Certainly, we learn to perceive our world by interaction with it. That much of the idea makes good sense, though it is not the whole story. And it is a curious irony that Ames, for whom past experience was of such theoretical importance, was at the same time the person who first called attention to aniseikonia. I cannot help feeling that the existence of this condition, which remains a visual handicap unless it is corrected by especially designed glasses, is important for showing the limits of past experience.

Lewin by this time was at M.I.T. and was deeply involved in the social-action research and group dynamics that his group there made so well known. He probably did not continue any sort of connection with Ames, but those

Hanover experiments seemed to me to be significant and interesting, partly, of course, because they fit right in with my own tendency to consider environmental factors lying beyond the retina and to consider the functioning of the whole perceptual system. The only point where I could not follow him was in his ideas about the role of experience, which he took over from H. L. F. von Helmholtz. But in spite of my disagreement with this aspect of Ames's theory, I cannot help feeling that his experiments should occupy a central place in "ecological" treatments of perception.

We had a dramatic demonstration of the effects of aniseikonia and of its correction by special eyeglasses in the case of the son of one of our Northampton neighbors. This boy, who was about twelve years old, had all sorts of unexplained problems. He did not try to play ball and do the things that other boys did at school. Some people thought that he suffered a kind of personality disturbance. When we got back to Northampton after the visit to Ames, we began to wonder whether his problems might not be related to aniseikonia; so we told his mother a little of what we had learned about it. She took him to Ames's clinic, where they diagnosed him as suffering from this eye problem and fitted him with glasses. His life was changed: he saw the world as most of us do, and he suddenly became a "normal" boy. This again demonstrated the limitations of the role of experience: how should one explain the change in this boy if experience is all-important? He had had ample experience with the objects of his environment. He had often met with difficulties in the course of interacting with them, but still he did not adjust his vision to take care of the riddles that they seemed to present to him. One would think that adaptation to retinas of unequal size would not pose greater problems than adjustment to upside-down lenses—and that, of course, has been effected to some extent, at least, in laboratory experiments. I do not know whether anybody has investigated adjustment to aniseikonic lenses in the same way.

We returned to Northampton from that Hanover visit during the summer of 1945 while our children were still away at camp, and I remember a small gathering that was reminiscent of my earlier days. I had been seeing two of my Hamburg friends, Heinz Werner and Martin Scheerer, off and on at psychological meetings. That spring, Martin had suggested that the three of us get together in the summer for some talks. Then he wanted to include his American-educated friend Solomon Asch in the group. By the time he made this suggestion, I knew that we could meet at our house in Northampton while the boys were still in camp. This was our first acquaintance with Asch, who, with his wife, Florence, has been very much part of our lives since, especially in recent years when they have spent several winters at the condominium near St. Augustine where Grace and I go. It was seven years before he published his well-known *Social Psychology*.

THE SEARCH FOR CONCEPTS: DISCOURAGEMENT

During this time my interest was coming to center more and more on questions related to interpersonal relations, and I was very much aware that the starting points for theorizing in this area were all around me: everybody has his not-yet-systematized thoughts about other people, his concepts about love and power, about benefit and harm. When I say everybody, I do not exclude rat psychologists. But how to grasp all that systematically? When I read nonscientific literature—novels, stories, plays—I often asked myself right away: "What do those expressions of ordinary language really imply? How do they relate to each other? Do they form a system in which each term has a defined place?"

The success of Lewin's psychology in representing action stimulated me anew to search for a conceptual tool that might be equally useful in clearing up the interrelations among these concepts whose opaqueness was bothering me. I soon saw that topology, as it had been developed by Lewin, did not help much with the description of processes going on between persons: there we often have to deal not with just one life space but with the relations and interactions between two or more life spaces. Frequently it is important to describe what one person thinks about another person's beliefs, hopes, and fears, or even to describe the effect of A's thoughts about what B thinks about C's wishes. I once described my difficulties with topology to Lewin; but he could not solve my problems; so I discarded topology.

However, I did not abandon the idea that I had learned from Lewin and Cassirer—namely, that in order to make progress in science, one has to find some way of fashioning a systematic representation of the material with which one is trying to deal. In the search for such a tool I even drove to New Haven with Grace through one autumn to attend Hull's weekly seminar at Yale. Hull's name is now almost forgotten except for a small circle of older psychologists, but during the thirties and the forties he was one of the most influential teachers. Every respectable psychologist who wanted to be taken seriously had to speak in terms of Hull's concepts of *drive reduction, goal responses,* and so on, based very much on experiments with rats. It may seem hard to believe now, but at that time there were many who thought seriously that Hull would be the American Newton of psychology. For a time there was a loose connection between Hull and Lewin, and some of Hull's students showed up at the yearly meetings of the Lewin group. Hull and Lewin were even planning to collaborate on some experiments.

In spite of vast differences in the content of what they thought of as psychology, they found common ground in their emphasis on the importance of using theory as a

144

starting point, Hull in what he called his hypothetico-deductive method and Lewin in his less formal maxim that "nothing is as practical as a good theory." We made the trips to New Haven in the hope that I might be able to use some of Hull's ideas for the representation that I needed in order to clear up my thinking about interpersonal relations. We enjoyed the atmosphere of the seminar meetings. Hull played the role of the tough-minded country boy who could not quite pronounce complicated words like "anthropology," for instance; he tried to show himself as the simple but honest scientist who did not fall for highfalutin mentalistic concepts.

I soon realized, however, that I could not learn much about the rich give-and-take of human experience from Hull's rat psychology. The empirical starting points of his experiments were too meager, and they derived from a too-simplistic theory. Today one has difficulty remembering the degree to which the laboratory rat dominated psychology at that time, when even such a humane and thoughtful man as Edward Tolman dedicated his 1932 book on the behavior of animals and men to the white rat—*Mus norwegicus albinus.*

As winter came, we gave up the long trips to New Haven, and I returned to the arduous work of clearing up the simple commonsense concepts that we use in thinking about people and their relations with each other. I did not yet have a definite plan to write a book dealing with such subjects; I just wanted to make my own thinking more definite and precise and to sharpen the mental tools that I had to use. I spent years explicating the meanings of words referring to everyday experiences. In these analyses my ever-present goal was to translate the content into concepts that could have definite places in a larger network of concepts. I give examples of that kind of inquiry in the first chapter of the book that I published in 1958 entitled *The Psychology of Interpersonal Relations.*

I think that I have already mentioned my attempts, while I was still in Hamburg, to define the words that we use for personality traits in the hope that they would provide an approach to greater clearness in my thinking about what goes on between people. Henry Murray's book *Explorations in Personality* came out in 1938, and I read it with great pleasure. It did not deal explicitly with relations between people, but his whole approach seemed to me more congenial and to capture aspects of human psychological functioning that were more significant and more realistic than the approaches of the abstract and academic rat psychology. It let in a breath of true life, and I soon succeeded in showing that eight of Murray's "needs" could be seen as a connected system, though Murray himself had not treated them that way.

When I came to write my own book, I intended to include that analysis, but somehow I failed to do so. I will try here to indicate a little of what I meant. If one uses the letter p to indicate the principal person and the letter o for the other person, then Murray's term "need aggression" can be presented as "*p wants p to cause something negative to o.*" "Nurturance" would be: "*p wants p to cause something positive to o.*" This means that one has an expression with three variables, each of which can have two values. Thus the expression can represent two times two times two—that is, eight—different meanings, each of which corresponds to one of Murray's needs.

It was only much later that I realized that I could not use Murray's concepts as such, though they were based on good observations and not on mere abstract speculations. I believe that the reasons Murray did not derive the full benefit from his descriptions of needs were, first, that he did not suspect that there might be systematic connections between them and, second, that in thinking about needs, he stuck to the simple paradigm of one entity—the person—and some kind of force within the person. The possibilities of descriptions become much more promising if one takes another paradigm—namely, a schema with two or more entities and some

146

kind of relation between them. In my attempts to fashion a symbolic language I experimented with both possibilities, and I found that the one using two or more entities with relations between them was the more efficient. I used it extensively for a number of years, and I found that such a system of notation serves to make the relationships between the concepts more obvious. I gave a brief description of it at the end of my 1958 book.

Of course, though the stimulus for devising this notation came from the usefulness that Lewin found in topology for a long time, my goal was more limited than Lewin's. Topological representations make use of mathematical relations that grow out of our ideas about space. They allow one to make predictions about what will happen given certain conditions. That is not true of the notation I suggested.

As I have said, I took material for these statements from a variety of sources, often even from stories for children. For instance, I made an analysis of Disney's story "Annabell, the Cow" and had it mimeographed for use in a seminar. It was a good starting point, since it described a variety of simple actions and their role in different little adventures. There was an amusing incident in regard to this story: one of the social scientists had been sitting in on my class. He had a father who shared his interest in psychology and who would be spending a few days in town. The son asked whether he might bring his father to the next meeting of the class, but when he learned the topic I planned to discuss, he changed his mind. "Annabell, the Cow" could have been too un-academic for someone of his father's generation.

In the same way, I worked over Aesop's fables; dramas by Racine, Ibsen, and many others; short stories; and also jokes. I may add here a quotation from my book: "The attitude that underlay these analyses was a feeling that there is a system hidden in our thinking about interpersonal relations, and that this system can be uncovered" (p. 14).

Perhaps I should add something about the relation of these analyses to what I have come to call commonsense psychology. I have often stressed the significance of the nonscientific psychology that we ordinarily use in our thinking about other people and ourselves. However, I did not take over commonsense notions without trying to refine or clarify them and, insofar as possible, to spell out their interrelations. In this sense, my treatment of interpersonal relations is not simply a matter of copying common sense but of using it as a step to something behind it.

Here I have moved forward to describe my thinking as it had developed by the end of our Northampton lives in 1947. It was only gradually that I came to have a firmer understanding of the direction in which I had to proceed and began to use new experiences as steps in that direction. At first I was conscious of this only in a limited sense. The 1944 paper ''Apparent Behavior,'' which I wrote with the help of Marianne Simmel, who was then one of my students at Smith College, belongs to this period in which I was working toward a goal that I was very much aware of although I had not yet fully defined it to myself. This study is based on descriptions made by groups of subjects of a short moving picture in which three geometric figures—a large triangle, a smaller triangle, and a circle—are seen to move about a field, in the center of which there is a rectangular enclosure with an opening at one side. As I planned the action of the film, I thought of the small triangle and the circle as a pair of lovers or friends, and I thought of the big triangle as a bully who intruded on them. The rectangle served as a room with a door, which could be opened or closed. The movements of the three characters were such that the two smaller ones in the end defeated and eluded the bully.

To make the film, we used an old moving-picture camera that could be driven manually. We had cardboard figures for our three characters and the room, and we placed them on a sheet of glass, on which the camera was focused from below. I figured out in advance exactly how far I had to move a figure to give the impression of slow or rapid movement, and we set out to work. I would place a figure;

Marianne would then make the exposure; I would move the figure to the next position; and so on. It took us about six hours, working in this exposure-by-exposure fashion, to make a film that gives a perception of lively movement and takes about three minutes to project. I still remember how pleased I was at my first showing of the film. And it has been impressive the way almost everybody who has watched it has perceived the picture in terms of human action and human feelings.

The film was a by-product of some work that Grace and I had done with children at the Clarke School. We were using a formboard test in which the child's task was to fit geometrical forms into the holes that had been cut in a wooden board of perhaps ten by fifteen inches. We had observed the children as they moved the forms about, sometimes trying one in a wrong hole, correcting errors, and trying another. We soon realized that just the movements of the hands holding the forms gave us a great deal of information about a child's puzzle-solving thought processes. We made moving pictures of some of these sessions so that we could study sequences of motions several times over. Then it occurred to me that the movements of the forms alone might be used to portray interpersonal situations.

It may be worthwhile to mention that while the geometric figures used in this film seem to have only the most tenuous relation to studies of physiognomic expression in which the face or handwriting is seen as "fitting" the personality, there is one aspect of the film that is perhaps more directly related to conventional assumptions regarding physiognomic expression: the circle was almost always seen as a female figure and the triangles as male.

The principal result of the analyses of the moving-picture descriptions was that movements or behavior, if you like, of even unchanging forms can produce an impelling impression of a network of interpersonal events and relations involving love, hate, power connections, fights, and happy reunions. I described these studies again in a paper that I gave called "Balance and Attribution" at a conference held at Dartmouth College in 1975. They were still meaningful then, thirty-some years later, long after I had been able to resolve more of my questions and more nearly to put my ideas together into a coherent form.

But already in 1944 they began to take shape in a second paper, "Social Perception and Phenomenal Causality," which I wrote after the film study and published the same year. In this paper I suggested that Wertheimer's unit-forming factors (similarity, proximity, etc.) may be not only "unit-forming" but also "causality-forming"—that is, that they often produce the impression of causality. This would mean, for instance, that two phenomena that are similar are more likely to be seen as connected by a causal relation than two that are dissimilar: for example, one is easily led to attribute a bad deed to a person who already has a bad reputation. Using these ideas, I came to formulations that would play an important part in my later work. The balance hypothesis is spelled out still more definitely in a 1946 paper entitled "Attitudes and Cognitive Organization."

I have often told how the idea of the balance hypothesis came to me when I was analyzing some of Spinoza's hypotheses in his *Ethics*. This truly remarkable book has two features that were especially relevant to my gropings at that time: first, it tries to represent its subject matter in a systematic way; and second, among other topics, it deals with interpersonal relations. I found that I could not use Spinoza's system, which he tried to fashion after Euclid's geometry and which did not fit my purposes. Nevertheless, his presentation was a great help to me because he grouped his propositions in a meaningful way. The long years when I had been trying out different ways of representing phenomena at last began to pay off. Spinoza's book contains a number of statements about love and hate which I could see made sense from my "commonsense" point of view; they gave the impression of being closely akin, though the way in which Spinoza tried to relate them to each other did not convince me.

All this time I was trying out a number of ways of representing these propositions, always working toward a representation that would show them all as instances of one general law. When I came to the idea of using the familiar unit-forming factors that I applied in the 1944 paper, the puzzle was more or less solved. I began to think in terms of a general tendency to prefer orderly and consistent arrangements of attitudes and unitlike connections to those that are less orderly and that can less easily be perceived as units.

It gave me great pleasure recently to find that Buddha mentioned what I would call two of the cases of imbalance as belonging among mankind's misfortunes: to be united with what one hates, and to be prevented from uniting with what one loves. These are cases of imbalance involving two items—a person and something or someone else. The relations become more varied if there are three items—for example, two persons and an object; but one can use the same general formula for specifying the conditions that lead to balance or imbalance.

I told Lewin about these thoughts during our visit to Ames at Hanover. I was eager to know what he would think of them, and I believed that if anyone would appreciate it, he would. I still remember exactly the place where we were when I tried to tell him what I meant. We were walking along a path that led through a meadow with scattered young trees and, in the background, blue hills. Lewin seemed to listen, he grunted a bit and nodded; but as soon as I stopped, he started talking about something else. He obviously had not understood at all what I had tried to explain. I gave up, feeling sad and lonely. If Lewin did not enter into such thoughts, would anybody, ever? I came to realize later that this was an especially crowded time in Lewin's life—a time when he was deeply involved in the complicated "action research" that was going on with his

M.I.T. group and when he was already perhaps feeling some anxieties about his health, which I remember his mentioning to me on one or more of our visits together that year. It is easy to understand that this was not the moment for him to move into a discussion of something that lay beyond his immediate pressures. However, I was very fortunate in the years ahead, after we had moved to Kansas, to have graduate students who would carry the ideas that I had sketched on paper into productive experimental studies. Still later, it gave me great pleasure, at one of the Lewin meetings, to hear Dorwin Cartwright and Frank Harary report their elegant versions of the balance hypothesis in terms of graph theory.

During the Second World War, I became more and more involved with teaching at Smith College. When Koffka died, I was asked to complete his first-semester course on gestalt psychology. Then, the next year I began teaching regularly in the Psychology Department with an introductory course in psychology and a seminar in experimental psychology. My students were undergraduate girls, pretty and very bright, but most of them were more interested in their boy friends than in psychology. There was little graduate work at Smith College, and I rarely had students like Marianne Simmel who had any interest in the ideas that I was concerned with. I enjoyed the teaching, but in the end it did not come close to the problems that I was trying to think through. All this, plus what had become part-time work at Clarke School, took up most of my time and energy during the academic year. I became more and more discouraged.

I was also frustrated with what I could do during the summer vacations to deal with the ideas about interpersonal relations that I was gradually developing. Somehow my brain does not seem to be a very efficient organ. It generates some acceptable products, but only after periods of leisurely dreaming and inactive somnolence. I am not a person of great energy, and the thinking that goes on in my head often seems to be without my personal participation. Nietzsche's words—that one should say, "It thinks," not, "I think"— seem very much to fit my case, and the life I was leading did not seem to give "it" much opportunity.

Gradually, during this period, I developed the idea of writing a book on interpersonal relations, but if I was to do that, I needed more unbroken stretches of free time. I went to New York and to Washington to try to get support from foundations, but everywhere came the same answer: there was nothing available for "conceptual research." A few of the people I talked with said that they, personally, would favor it; the time would come when help would be available—perhaps in five years—but at present it would not be possible to persuade a committee to accept the kind of proposal that I was talking about.

The result of all this was that I felt cornered and became the victim of attacks of anxiety. It is true that they gave me some new insights and were perhaps worthwhile in a way, but on the whole it was a rather unpleasant way of learning about myself. These attacks always came on when I was lying down for an afternoon nap or for a night's sleep; therefore, even sleep was no longer an escape from what was troubling me. I often formulated my situation or my fate in a kind of picture, partly to realize more clearly what was happening, partly to exaggerate and make fun of it—a way of handling what is unpleasant in life perhaps. The picture accompaniment to the attacks of anxiety was taken from the old story of Prometheus, chained to a rock, with an eagle coming every day to feed on his liver. Though I did not really compare myself to this hero, there was always a ferocious bird that, when I lay down to sleep, came and hacked away at my heart and liver with great gusto. I am sure that this annoying image stemmed from the old Greek saga. I tried to fight the bird off in different ways, but it was very persistent and merciless. It even seemed to me that the more I struggled to repel it, the fiercer its attacks became.

My lack of success in getting rid of the bird made me question my approach; so I went back to the philosophy of my earlier years. I asked: "Why do I defend myself so strenuously? After all, I am not so important. Other people are much more important, and there are many more of them!" So I tried to be friendly to the fierce bird. I said to him: "Come on. I am at your service." This cordial invitation had a dramatic effect. It seemed that the one thing against which it was helpless, the one thing it could not stand, was being treated in a familiar way and without respect. The ferocious bird became disgusted and suddenly flew away. When I tried to fill my thinking with the idea "I am not so important" and when I told myself that it did not matter whether or not all those unripe thoughts that I felt growing ever came to fruition, I would feel a sudden relaxation in the region of my heart. My attacks of anxiety stopped. These experiences made me believe very much in a relation between egocentricity, tension, and anxiety, something that is doubtless familiar to people who deal with such problems, recently to people who work with biofeedback.

This was the first time that I had become aware of changes in tension. Since then I have learned more about how to recognize them and how to influence them. I know the pleasant feeling when the blood is flowing out into my limbs and when relaxation is spreading over my body. I try to get this feeling every day as I am going to sleep. The motif "I am not important" still has a place in my mental equipment. I would guess that it has saved me some heartache and frustration, and it is also a balance to counteract the opposed force of my own importance that I have in common with most people.

I should like to add to these remarks about the anxiety attacks that there was the possibility of a mere physiological contributing factor, and that was my smoking. I was never what one would call a heavy smoker. At the time about which I am writing I usually smoked half a pack of cigarettes a day and one or two small cigars with my afternoon tea. However, it was difficult to ventilate my large third-floor study thoroughly. The windows were small and not easy to open, and the air in the room was rather heavy with smoke and with the dust that inevitably comes from accumulations of books. Eventually, I cut down on my smoking and aired the room more often. These measures may also have contributed to the abatement of my troubles.

For a long time during the later years of my Northampton stay I also allowed myself to play with another picture that seemed to illustrate my life situation, one that probably had no relationship to that of the predatory bird. It must happen that when a person's mind is constantly engaged in working out plans for a longer treatise, he goes on for a long time with little to show for what he is doing, even though he knows that he is working hard all the time in his own way. The people around him may not realize what is going on; his sitting around and thinking and making notes may seem to be just a matter of loafing and idle self-indulgence. This was more or less my situation during these years, and I often had a bad conscience about the fact that I did not contribute more to the daily chores that had concrete, visible effects. On the whole, members of my family were amazingly understanding, but every so often I felt that they were at the point of losing patience with my apparent idleness. I illustrated my situation for myself by making up a fable about what I called "the invisible load." I imagined a group of people setting out on a trek across a desert, all of them carrying packs. Most of these packs were obviously heavy, but there was one person who seemed to have only a small, light sack. He himself knew that actually he was bearing a heavy burden, something that would be of great value to all of them when they arrived at their destination; but nobody else could see that this man's burden was even heavier than those of the others. This was the "invisible burden." Thus, half making fun of myself, I expressed my situation in different ways.

155

But I should return to the narrative of our Northampton days and tell how it came about that we left this town where so much had been so pleasant. Gradually, as the frustrations of my situation wore me down, Paul Nathan, who was family physician as well as close friend to us and to others in the Smith College community, began to worry about me. Mrs. Neilson warned Grace that I might be on the verge of a serious illness. She said that we must at least get away for that summer (1946), and she went so far as to ask us to let her pay the rent for a cottage on the ocean. We went to Martha's Vineyard, off the Massachusetts coast, and took a small house with an open garage, which I used as a study where I worked regular hours in the fresh, salt air. Lewin and his wife came for a visit and stayed with kind friends of ours who had their own, a much larger, summer home within easy driving distance. This visit was a delight but also a frustration, because Lewin was so busy reading proof on an article that there was almost no time when we could discuss theoretical problems as we had done in the old days. When he was not working, he wanted to be out of doors, especially teaching our three sons more than they had known before about the small sailboat that we shared with friends.

But a visit that Lewin made with his two children to Northampton over the days after Thanksgiving more than made up for the frustration of Martha's Vineyard. On the first day, all of us climbed nearby Mt. Tom. On another day, Lewin and I went off by ourselves into the woods and had a good talk on the problems that had meant so much to both of us. This was the last time that I saw Lewin, but a visit that he had with Grace in January may have been related to the relaxed mood of that day. My back had been giving me trouble again, and I was in a Boston hospital in an attempt to get the problem in hand, while Grace, in the meantime, was staying with the family of the physician who had arranged the hospital stay for me. They were old friends who lived in a suburb near where the Lewins had settled. One evening,

Grace had dinner with the Lewins—Kurt must have picked her up in his car as he drove home from his office. Gerti Lewin had to go out soon after dinner, but Grace stayed a little while before Kurt drove her back to the place where she was staying. She remembers that he paced up and down the room, scolding that if I would only apply for an experimental grant, which he was sure I could get with his backing, everything would be simple. His idea was that the grant would pay for a couple of graduate students and a secretary to handle the experiments while I sat in my office and worked on the book that I wanted to write.

Grace doubtless tried to explain to him that such a plan would not fit my temperament—that I had to work things out in my own slow way without feeling responsible for what was going on in a laboratory. The discussion ended with his telling her how he himself planned to pull out of the "action research" that had kept him going at such a fierce pace those last years and to go back to theoretical problems. He added almost triumphantly that Roger Barker (see p. 155) and I would both be pleased. Of course, the apparent difference between his advice to me and his own plans boiled down to the fact that he, as a professor at M.I.T., was relatively free to arrange his time as he chose. On the other hand, a grant tied to an experimental study was probably the only way for me, as an associate professor at Smith College, to get the time I needed for what I wanted to do. I would guess that it was Lewin's decision to go back to theoretical work that put him in the mood to have that talk during the Thanksgiving visit. But he was never to carry out the plan. Within a month he had died. Shocking, saddening as this was, it was in a way not altogether surprising. With his enormous creative energy and his powers of concentration, Lewin had lived the lives of three men during the span allotted to him.

Another visitor that summer at Martha's Vineyard was Rudi Arnheim, a friend from my Berlin days. He was deep in studies of art, based to a large extent on ideas of gestalt psychology. I greatly enjoyed discussing all sorts of problems with him. Still more important, as regards my immediate situation and difficulties, was a visit from Mrs. Koffka, who was staying in the region with the Köhlers. She knew what I was trying to do and that in spite of a good summer I felt that I would never get the time I needed in order to write the book that by now I had definitely in mind. She had an immediate solution for the problem—and I have remained grateful to her for suggesting it. She said that I should apply for a Guggenheim fellowship, and she said that Köhler was on the board of the Guggenheim Foundation. He knew my work and would certainly back my application. We knew that a year on a Guggenheim would be a tight squeeze for us financially. Those fellowships were more or less tailored to the needs of academic people on sabbatical leave from their colleges or universities and who therefore were receiving half their usual salaries. I, who had been on irregular appointment at Smith College during most of my time there, was not in line for a sabbatical leave. But the possibility of a whole year of uninterrupted work toward the book was an intoxicating thought, too good to pass up. We knew that we would manage somehow or other. At the end of the summer we went back to Northampton, refreshed and hopeful and with a lease on the cottage on Martha's Vineyard for the summer of 1947. But much was to happen before that summer, and we did not see Martha's Vineyard again for twenty years.

THE MOVE TO KANSAS

The first thing was to get the Guggenheim application in. With the possibility of free time ahead, I attacked the problems of interpersonal relations with new hope and energy. A new and pleasant feature of our lives then was having Roger and Louise Barker, whom we had known at Lewin meetings for more than ten years, settle in Worcester, fifty miles east of Northampton. Roger was at Clark University as G. Stanley Hall Professor. By spring the four of us were meeting somewhere between Worcester and Northampton every few weeks for dinner. We always had lots to talk about, from psychology to children, their three and our three. It was at one of these meetings that Roger asked whether we would consider moving to Kansas, a thought that certainly had never occurred to us. He explained that he had been offered the chairmanship of the Psychology Department at the University of Kansas. There had been some sort of administrative upheaval, and several positions were open. He would like to go if he could get some of his colleagues—by which he meant people from the old Lewin group—to go with him. We realized right away that this would give me exactly what I needed after the years at Smith College and Clarke School—an opportunity to teach graduate students, with whom I could develop my own thoughts, as well as to present the basic ideas of the field. I accepted right away, as casually as I had decided at the Hamburg celebration to come to America.

However, one obstacle developed: I had just had my fifty-first birthday, and the Kansas Board of Regents, which controlled the university, had a rule against hiring a new faculty member over the age of fifty. All this was finally worked out, and certainly the fact that by that time I had been awarded a Guggenheim fellowship helped make it possible to get the fifty-year rule set aside. A compromise was worked out by which I was to be excluded from Kansas' state retirement system but receive a small addition to my salary instead.

The regents had another rule that might have added to our financial problems that year—one against having more than one member of the same family on the university payroll at a time; however, it had opportunely been suspended just when we moved. Enrollment at the university, probably at most universities in the country, had increased with the return of veterans following the end of World War II, and qualified wives were needed as teachers, at least in Kansas. This meant that Grace could be a member of the department, and her salary helped to make up for the limited amount of the Guggenheim stipend. In the end the wives were needed for the second year of our Kansas lives.

As I look back on our decision to move to Kansas, I recall an anecdote that concerns Paul Lieder, a professor of English at Smith College. He was our next-door neighbor, and it was said that he kept open house, with sherry for adults, Coca Cola for children, and dog biscuits for canine visitors. At that time, Herbert Davis was president of the college, and he had a big Labrador retriever who was a frequent guest at Paul's apartment. Just about this time I saw the dog sitting on the sidewalk outside, and I leaned over to pat him, as I must have done many times before. He turned around and, quick as a flash, bit me in the wrist so that, even with my coat sleeve for protection, I was bleeding a little. I recalled this incident as we were saying goodby to our friends before we left, and I told them that there was an Austrian saying that when the president's dog starts biting you, it is time to leave.

The three boys were told about the move as soon as matters were fairly well settled. It was John who spoke first, "But we won't have any roots." However, the fact that for the first time we would probably have a house of our own instead of living year-round in a rented house, as we had in Northampton, and the excitement of the move soon made them enthusiastic. By the end of June 1947 we were on our way. Roger Barker had already made plans to teach in Oregon for the summer, so we could start our Kansas life in the large house that the Barkers had rented for the year, taking in one new member of the staff after another as he arrived and hunting for a house to buy for ourselves during the first days.

We soon found the house that we wanted—a red Victorian "mansion" with large rooms, high ceilings, and marble fireplaces, one whose price was within our range, since houses of that period were out of favor in Lawrence just then. Even so, the purchase was difficult, because the banks required a relatively large down payment on an older house. However, one of Grace's uncles and a friend helped out with loans, and we were soon settled into the home where we would live until our sons had left for college and adventures beyond. I had a big corner room upstairs with a view of the nearby Kaw River, and there was enough space so that the boys could come and go as noisily as they liked with their friends without disturbing me. I put up the bookcases in my study and settled down to work. Our sons were soon busy in their new schools, and Grace began teaching in the Department of Psychology.

As I write about these Kansas years that began more than thirty years ago, I find it harder to visualize what went on than in some of the much earlier periods of my life. However, one incident of our move remains in my mind because it was related to that period in Kansas history. Kansas was one of the few states that had maintained its "dry" status after the Eighteenth Amendment and the Volstead Act had been repealed. When we packed our books in Northampton, we used the sturdy boxes in which liquor stores received their stock, one hundred thirty some boxes in all. They arrived by railroad freight later than the furniture, which traveled more expensively by truck. When we went to the railway station to see about having them delivered, not thinking what their labels would suggest in Kansas, we found the freight agent unhappily bent over the great array of boxes. We told him what they contained, but it was obviously his duty to examine each box. Finally he thought of a solution: he stood erect to ask, "Mr. Heider, would you be willing to swear that none of those boxes contains liquor?" I could do that with a free conscience, for we had

Grace and Fritz Heider in September 1955

Heinz Werner, Solomon Asch, and Tamara Dembo,
1955

known in advance that Kansas was a dry state, and we had given away the last item of our small cellar before we set out.

We soon felt at home in the friendly little city to which we had moved. Roger Barker, a man of the Midwest, had felt hemmed in by the hills of New England and had described the feeling that Lawrence gave him of great open spaces and a main street that seemed to go on endlessly to the south. We had loved the hills that we were leaving behind but were agreeably surprised that Lawrence was not as entirely flat as some of our Northampton friends had warned us that it would be. As a matter of fact, there was a fairly steep little hill, exaggeratedly known as Mt. Oread, in the center of the city. This hill had been set aside for a future university as Lawrence was being platted. From it in one direction one could see the river, on which the city was located, and in the other, beyond roofs and trees, one could see fields and woods. It was also pleasant to find ourselves in a place where town-gown tensions were almost completely absent, partly of course because the university was coeducational. Almost every business and professional man in the city had attended it at some time and was proud of belonging to it, something that obviously could not be the case with a college for women like Smith.

The city had been founded by a group of pre-Civil War antislavery pioneers under the auspices of the Massachusetts Emigrant Aid Company; it was named for the family that had also founded Lawrence, Massachusetts. This was a period when settlers from both North and South were being rushed to the region to determine whether Kansas and Nebraska would be admitted to the Union as Free States or as Slave States. Lawrence was officially settled in 1854. We remember that when it celebrated its centennial, our sons were privately unimpressed: Northampton, where they had been born, was celebrating its three hundredth anniversary that same year, and St. Augustine, which they had visited, was almost four hundred years old.

We especially enjoyed the pleasant atmosphere of our relatively small department. Those of us who had been associated with Lewin, and our wives, had known each other for some years, at least from meetings of the topological group. Roger Barker, who had taken his doctorate with Walter Miles at Stanford, and Herbert Wright, who had studied with Donald Adams at Duke, had been together as postdoctoral fellows in Lewin's Iowa laboratory. The Barkers, Roger and Louise, and the Wrights, Herbert and Lorene, soon selected Oskaloosa, a small town near Lawrence, and moved there to pioneer a study of "psychological ecology," which attempts to describe the psychologically relevant features of the environment in which people live. They point out that different environmental settings—as, for example, church, drugstore, swimming pool—are experienced as either demanding or coercing specific kinds of behavior.

One of the younger members of the group who had been in the department before we came chose to throw his lot in with the newcomers, Anthony Smith. He and his wife, Barbara, were soon good friends.

A year later, Martin Scheerer and his wife, Constance, joined us. I had known Martin while he was still a student at Hamburg. He had worked with Stern and Cassirer and so was intimately familiar with gestalt psychology. His thesis, published in 1931, was an interesting critique of gestalt theories from the Hamburg point of view which stressed Stern's personalism and Cassirer's neo-Kantianism. He maintained that gestalt psychology is wrong in treating psychological phenomena as physical processes and that it neglects the dimension of meaning: it confuses intentionality with a process in inorganic nature. This criticism, of course, is directed against certain general underpinnings of the theory and accepts most of the brilliant observations and experiments that are generally known as the contributions of gestalt theory. For me, personally, Martin was a very welcome connection with my European past, especially with my

Martin Scheerer, Erik Wright, and Beatrice Wright, December 1956

days in Berlin and Hamburg. He was a close friend until his sudden death in the fall of 1961.

The next year, Alfred Baldwin, another friend from the topological meetings, joined us. He had been a graduate student at Harvard when Lewin was a visiting professor there a few years earlier.

In 1951 Beatrice and Erik Wright came. They were graduate students with Lewin in Iowa when Roger Barker and Herbert Wright were postdoctoral fellows there. Beatrice had worked with Roger on a book about psychological aspects of physical handicaps, while Erik had added an M.D. and a residency at the Medical School of the University of California to the Ph.D. that he had obtained at Iowa with Lewin. He remained a warm friend to our family and to many, a tower of strength in the university and the community until his unbelievable sudden death in the spring of 1981. Erik became the first director of the clinical program of

Roger Barker, 1975

Herbert Wright, 1975

the Department of Psychology, with Martin a dynamic teacher in that area, while I, after my Guggenheim year was over, taught a survey course for graduate students known as Advanced General and soon a course in the history of psychology.

Another aspect of our life in Kansas was our relationship with members of the staff of the psychoanalytically oriented Menninger Foundation in Topeka. David Rapaport, head of the Research Department, was someone we had met several years before when he had paid a visit to Smith College and had attended a meeting of Koffka's seminar. He welcomed our coming, and we were soon friends, getting together with him and Sybille ("Bille") Escalona every few weeks for discussions. Bille's parents had been friends of the Lewins in Berlin, and Bille had spent her first years in this country with the Lewin family in Iowa City.

We also came to know George Klein and his wife, Bessie, a gifted artist. I think of George as one of the psychologists who most completely understood the different aspects of my thinking and who, incidentally, was to play an important part in the publication both of my book on interpersonal relations and, the next year, of a series of papers going back to "Ding und Medium" in its English translation.

I may also mention Margaret Brenman, another therapist at the Menninger Foundation, and her husband, William Gibson, a delightful man who was then not quite settled in a career but who was busy writing (poetry and plays) and also playing in a jazz orchestra. It was during our first year in Kansas that things began to fall into place for him. First, the Oxford University Press published a book of his poems; then a well-known producer came from New York to see the University Theater put on one of his plays. By this time he was well on his way to becoming the playwright who is known for *Two-for-the-Seesaw*, *The Miracle Worker*, and much more during the years that followed.

In that same year came the breakup of the Topeka group. Rapaport and the Gibsons left Topeka for the Austen-Riggs Foundation in Massachusetts, and George Klein left later for New York University. Bille Escalona succeeded Rapaport as head of the Research Department, and Grace, after the nepotism rules were reinstated at the university in the fall of 1949, worked half time with her and Mary Leitch, a child analyst, on a study of the range of behavior that could be observed in a group of "normal, healthy, well-developing infants." Another change took Bille to Yale, and later to the Albert Einstein School of Medicine, and brought Gardner and Lois Murphy to the Menninger Foundation in 1952. Gardner, a warm, wise, and effective person whose broad interests had made him a major figure in important fields of psychology, became director of the Research Department. Lois, a creative pioneer in child psychology, began the Coping Project. This was basically a study of the strengths of children, of the ways in which the average, run-of-the-mill child handles the problems that every child meets. Most of the subjects of this study were children who had been seen as babies in the Escalona-Leitch project, and Grace, who had known them and their families, either firsthand or through project records, served as a connecting link between the two studies. Lois Murphy was a stimulating researcher, and the collaboration with her congenial group continued for almost eight years. One happy aspect of it was the friendship that developed between the two Murphys and the two of us.

I may mention a special debt that we owe to Gardner. Grace had accumulated graduate credits from her work with Koffka at Smith College and had published results of work that she had done in his laboratory, as well as papers alone and jointly with me in our Clarke School monographs, and had even taught graduate courses during her two years in the university's Department of Psychology; but she had never completed a doctorate. One day, Gardner sent a message to her by Lois, asking why she did not finish work for a degree at the University of Kansas: she could not get any more raises unless she did, he explained. By the next week she had begun a required course in statistics, something that certainly had not been talked about in Koffka's relatively European laboratory. Our sons, by that time, were mostly away from home; and the half-to-three-quarters-time schedule, which had seemed wise while she was keeping house for a family and commuting to Topeka, allowed her to have a doctorate in hand when it proved very useful a few years later.

Another friend of our early Kansas years was Edward Robinson, a member of the Philosophy Department. Edward was involved during much of this time in making a translation of Heidegger's *Sein und Zeit*, which was published in 1962. This bachelor's dinners brought us into contact with a wide range of faculty members, especially younger philosophers as they joined his department. It was only after his untimely death in a traffic accident that we learned that my cousin Stephan Philippovich had married a second cousin of Edward's, a tenuous connection to be sure, but one that we would have enjoyed together if we had realized it sooner.

There was another incident during our first spring at the university that belongs among the coincidences that are bound to occur in the course of a long life. It was related to what I mentioned earlier in this history, that my father's father had been dentist to the Habsburg family. That spring there was an announcement that the Archduke Otto, then claimant to the imperial throne of Austria, would give a lecture on campus. At first I said that I would not go, for my Uncle Karl and especially my father had been anti-Habsburg in their leanings, and I had inherited their outlook as I grew up in the more or less rebellious province of Styria. But then my curiosity overcame my negative feelings, and I wanted to hear the young man; so we bought tickets and attended the lecture. I found that I liked him, and I asked Grace (who took to telephoning more comfortably than I did) to see whether there was any time during his two- or three-day stay when I might meet him. The wife of the dean who had introduced us to Lawrence told Grace that he was staying at the chancellor's house and urged her to call the chancellor's wife, Mrs. Malott. It seemed that he did not have a free half-hour on his schedule, but Mrs. Malott, in her warm way, said, "Come and have breakfast with us tomorrow." We did, and it was a pleasant meal, with the chancellor, Deane

Malott, as though with one foot in present-day America and one back in history, saying, "Won't you have more scrambled eggs, Archduke?" and then asking him when he had come closest to gaining the throne.

The breakfast, of course, did not last long, and as I told the archduke goodby, I said, "My ancestors have caused your ancestors much pain." There was a sudden stiffening of the atmosphere in the group at the door—"Is he a descendant of an anarchist or what?" must have flashed through their minds. But I continued immediately, of course, by explaining that my grandfather had been dentist to the family of the Emperor Franz Joseph.

Over the years, as one can expect in academic circles, came visits to the university or to us personally of friends from Northampton. One memorable visitor was Antonio Borgese, of the old Ladies' and Gentlemen's Club at Smith College. He was by this time a professor at the University of Chicago and had been invited by the Humanities Committee at Kansas for a two-week stay, to give several lectures and to visit with classes. When his coming was announced, we wrote to ask whether he remembered the Heiders of his Northampton days, and we received a cordial response. The chairman of the committee brought him to our house for lunch the first day. He seemed very frail, and after an evening or two of dinner parties, he decided that he was happier having quiet evenings with us; so he refused the invitations that were offered to him. Each day when we finished our meal, he talked until he was in the mood to be taken to his hotel.

In retrospect we regret that tape recorders were not then available so that we could have preserved those monologues. They must have been like the conversations with Goethe that Eckermann wrote up. Even the boys were fascinated, and one of them asked whether he might bring his girl friend, which he did without disturbing the atmosphere of the occasion. I remember especially the evening

170

when Borgese talked about the Roman Catholic Church, which he seemed to have left behind when he emigrated from Mussolini's Italy. He said that the Church was not a woman with whom you have an affair; he had left her, but he would go back to her before he died. It was like the fifth-century St. Augustine crying out, "Not yet, Oh Lord." We read of Borgese's death the next year, but we never knew what was his final relationship with the Church.

The Kansas years also brought new contacts with European psychologists who came to spend time in the department—among others, Alastair Weir from Glasgow, Joseph Nuttin from Louvain, Jan Smedslund from Norway, and Ivo Kohler from Innsbruck.

The meetings of the Lewin group continued, in the late summers after the American Psychological Association changed the time of its annual meeting from the Christmas holidays to August. There was one at Philipsburg, Pennsylvania, at which I was the principal speaker for the whole period of two or three days. I remember especially Leon Festinger's friendly but combative disagreement at each point I made, and finally the rump session on a Sunday morning, when many of the group had already left for the committee meetings that come just before the meetings of the association. Leon and a few others were there, and we were having a final round when he broke out with, "Now I understand what it is all about," or something to that effect. This was in 1958, when my book was just coming out but before many people had read it, I am sure.

To go back to my first year in Kansas, when the Guggenheim fellowship allowed me to devote all of my time to thinking and to writing what I was becoming certain would be a book on interpersonal relations. I have mentioned that I had collected a formidable mass of examples that seemed relevant to a study of events involving two or more persons. These events were described in common-sense language, and I felt that they needed to be mulled over and meditated on. Always what kept me going was the persisting conviction that these simple, everyday words did not represent a mass of chaotic, unrelated meanings, but that in spite of the many different kinds of relations among them, there must be some sort of system of which they were parts, even though it is not quite visible at first glance.

And I suppose the guiding example that I emulated all this time was Lewin's attempt to represent actions by making use of some sort of mathematical discipline—in his case, for a long time, of topology. I had soon found that topology would not solve my problems in dealing with more than one person, but I have the feeling that it stayed with me as a model for the kind of thing that I wanted to do. I cannot say that I intended to produce a "theory of interpersonal relations." What I was trying to do at that point was to elucidate these excellent commonsense descriptions of behavior by bringing some sort of conceptual clarity to them. One way of studying them seemed to be to line them up and then look at each one in the light of the others. The poet Donne has said, "No man is an island"; so one can also say of these concepts dealing with interpersonal relations, "They are not islands; they show their full meaning only in interaction with others." There is a complicated network, a system hidden in these seemingly simple concepts, that is a wonderful instrument for capturing subtle meanings of human happenings and states.

For example, when I want to get a clearer idea of the concept of "ought," I am not satisfied with just steeping myself in thoughts about this word "ought" as such. I try to make some mental experiments to get an idea of what I mean when I say that a person ought to do x but does not do it. And then, what are the relations between "ought" and the possibility concepts? Can one say, "He ought to do x" when x is impossible for him to do?

All this is part of what I was doing during that first year in Kansas. By the fall of 1948, however, when I began teaching, the book was still not finished, though a great deal had fallen into place in my own thinking. One boost came when Alfred Baldwin joined the department and began reading the rough drafts of chapters of the still unnamed volume. He had them mimeographed and sent them out to a few people who might be interested. Then, one summer, Ann and Sidney Hook, friends from our Vermont days, stopped on a trip west. Sidney and I, of course, talked about my work and my discouragement about getting the book into the final form in which I would want it to appear. Sidney, knowing more about these things than I did from the vantage point of his New York life, suggested what had never occurred to me, that once having had a Guggenheim fellowship, it would be a simple matter to get a second one in order to complete the work that was under way from the first; so that is what I did. By this time, other foundations were also more open to my nonexperimental approach, and I was able to get funding for an assistant to help with the final preparation of the chapters that were to form the book. Here I had incredible good fortune: Beatrice Wright—who, like Grace, was not allowed to teach because of nepotism rulings but was not yet deeply into work toward her own book— agreed to help me on a half-time basis for the year, and the task came to an end.

Then came the problem of getting the book published. A university press, whose editor one of my former students knew, agreed to consider it; but the copy that was sent to him somehow got lost. We sent a second copy and waited. Then a commercial press considered it but rejected it, we heard later, as being "nothing but common sense." About this time, George Klein, who was now living in New York, stepped into the picture and suggested John Wiley & Sons, whose psychology editor was someone whose judgment he valued. By the summer of 1957 Wiley, Knopf, and the original university press all had copies for consideration. Wiley offered to report on a certain date, and I gave that date as a deadline to the other two. Wiley called during our lunch hour that day, accepting the book enthusiastically—George Klein was probably one of their readers. Soon came Knopf, saying that their principal reader for books in this field was abroad and asking me to hold off my decision for two weeks. Shortly after that came a favorable call from the university press. I accepted Wiley's offer, and the book was on its way, appearing in 1958.

TRAVELS AND RETIREMENT

Now began what was in some ways a new chapter for us. For a good many years, life had followed a preplanned course. Except for the time of the two Guggenheim fellowships, the academic year had meant work that, however interesting and rewarding in itself, had been an interruption of what I most wanted to do just then—to clear up ideas in my own slow way and to shape the thinking that in the end produced the book on interpersonal relations. The all-too-short summers had always been times when I tried, some years more successfully than others, to push ahead. Only once had I broken this pattern, at the end of our second year in Kansas, when Ernest Hilgard, then chairman of the Psychology Department at Stanford, asked me to teach in the summer session. The opportunity of seeing more of the country, especially the West, was too much to resist, partly perhaps because it took me back to my father's old thought of moving to California after the 1906 earthquake. We and the three boys, by then fourteen, twelve, and nine, drove out, camping as we went. For my psychological thinking the most important product of the summer was the work that I did for a course in the history of psychology, which certainly deepened my own understanding and also provided the groundwork for teaching that I did during the rest of my years in the Kansas department. It was also an opportunity to spend time with Egon and Else Brunswik, then at nearby Berkeley, and to talk with Tolman, whom I had met at topological meetings. And, of course, we enjoyed our contacts with members of the Stanford department and others who were there for the summer as I was.

In the meantime, the book was being read, and reviews had appeared. I remember especially one by Harold H. Kelley of UCLA, who mentioned *balance* and *attribution* as topics of special importance. As the book became known, there were invitations to visit other departments. In the spring of 1959 I taught at Cornell, filling in for my old friend James Gibson, who was spending the year at the Princeton Institute of Higher Studies. One of my memories of that year is of the nightmarish drive from Lawrence to Ithaca. I had strained my back once more while trying to shovel snow not long before we were to leave. It was later that year that I saw Dr. Travell and began really to understand what I could and could not do. Until the last day of the trip, Grace had to do all the driving. It was midwinter, January, and weather reports gave us the information that a blizzard was on the way, moving from west to east, so she drove as many hours as she dared each day to keep ahead of it. We finally made it and were soon settled into an apartment fairly near the campus. I might add that this was the year when Grace was completing her Kansas doctorate and that she had to make several trips back during the semester, practically commuting, we felt.

We enjoyed the new setting, and I had good talks with other Cornell psychologists, especially Alfred Baldwin. He and Nina Lambert and their collaborators were working on a social-psychological experiment that was published in 1969 as a *Child Development Monograph*. I still feel that it is a magnificent piece of work and many years ahead of much contemporary research. I have special regard for it because it probes aspects of naïve, commonsense psychology and because it formulates a theory that makes use of a kind of calculus in an innovative way. I should also mention that the theory took care of 96 percent of the variance in the experimental results.

In the spring of 1960, after a year at home in Kansas, Grace and I set out for Europe, where Oslo was to be our headquarters for two summers and the academic year between. I was on a Fulbright fellowship, which, like the Guggenheim, had a stipend tailored to the needs of a faculty member on sabbatical leave from his own university; and Grace had a research fellowship from the National Institute of Mental Health in Washington to enable her to finish writing up work that she had done with Lois Murphy at the Menninger Foundation and to participate in the work of a child-research laboratory connected with the University of Oslo. The two stipends gave us a comfortable margin for life in Oslo and for travel in Europe, which let me renew old contacts on that side of the Atlantic. During the first summer we attended the meeting of the International Psychological Congress at Bonn, where old friends from both America and Europe had gathered.

Stephan, who had finished a second year at the University of Minnesota and was to be at Durham University in England while we were in Norway, met us after the congress at a nearby city and went with us to Austria, to have his first glimpse of my homeland and the relatives who were still living. It had been twenty-eight years since Grace and I had made our trip in 1932. In between had come the political changes of the years after Hitler's rise in early 1933, when, aside from the fact that by 1935 we began to be tied down with small children, we did not especially care to go. Then came World War II and the difficult recovery years for Europe; then years when we had one or sometimes two sons away at school or college and could not afford a trip. We had been glad that the two older boys had been able to go earlier without us: Karl had been awarded a traveling fellowship when he graduated from Harvard in 1956, and after a slow trip through Asia, he had spent a year on an Austrian government fellowship at the University of Vienna, the third Karl Heider of my family to study there. John, who had taken a year off between preparatory school and college, had spent part of the time vagabonding in Europe, with the home of my cousin Stephan Philippovich and his American wife as a welcoming haven whenever he needed a respite. Karl and John had both come to know Gusti and Mizi and the family of my half sister Gertraud, and they had stayed at the Feistritz house, where Gusti made his home after retiring. All three sons had studied German in school or college, and each was soon able to talk comfortably with the relatives in their own language.

Gusti, by this time, was ninety-two, and I remember one morning when Stephan and Grace and I set off from the house without telling Gusti what we had planned, for we assumed that a real walk would be too much for him. We had not gone far before we found him sitting on a fence, and he asked whether he might join us. He suggested a path through the woods that led us up and down hill. The three of us were more or less worn out by the time we returned, but he seemed as fresh as when we had started.

The year in Norway brought us new contacts that we enjoyed, both with Norwegian psychologists and with Americans who were there, as we were, on various kinds of appointments for the year. All the Norwegian academic people spoke fluent English, and the seminar that I gave for psychologists and sociologists was conducted in English, which, since the war, had replaced German as the language that was most frequently learned in school. Memories of the German occupation of Norway during the war were still fresh and bitter at the time of our stay. It was mentioned that I, being originally Austrian, was welcome, but that they would have hesitated to invite me if I had been German.

International Psychological Congress, Bonn, Germany, 1960.
Left to right, Ludwig Kardos, Philipp Lersch, Fritz Heider, R.
Meili

Grace once, after our return from Austria, made a slip and left a neighborhood store with "auf Wiedersehen" instead of the Norwegian goodby. The storekeeper drew himself up and said coldly, in Norwegian of course, "You are German." She hastily answered in his own language, "No, no, I am American"; and the atmosphere was once more friendly. We both worked on Norwegian during our time in the country, Grace beginning with a summer course for foreign students at the university and I mostly from reading newspapers and books for boys that we found in the library of the people from whom we had rented the apartment where we spent the year. Our first knowledge of the American election of 1960 came from a newspaper headline to the effect that the Scandinavian-American vote had elected John F. Kennedy president. We also went a good deal to the Norwegian-language repertory theaters in Oslo, where the management supplied us with advance copies of the play of the week.

There was often Ibsen, of course, and some plays translated from the English. I remember *The Great Kean* from London and William Gibson's *Miracle Worker* from New York. Grace used the Norwegian dictionary to be sure of the words on her grocery list each time she went shopping, and she found that the storekeepers were helpful whenever she thought of something while she was out that she had failed to look up. Once she wanted vanilla extract, and she tried the English word for a start—sometimes the English and the Norwegian would be similar enough so that the storekeeper could make a correct guess. This time he found himself helpless; so he appealed to the half-dozen other customers in the store. One of them suggested the correct Norwegian word, which was similar but had quite different vowel sounds and accent. The storekeeper delightedly ran and brought back vanilla beans. Grace was able to explain in her limited vocabulary, "No, vanilla like water"; and this time the attempt was successful. He answered the equivalent of "vanilla drops" and reached for the bottle that she wanted.

We spent the Christmas holidays, along with Stephan, in Sicily, making stops in Switzerland and Italy both coming and going. I had given a lecture in London just before, and I had started on the trip somewhat under the weather with a light influenza, but it was a rich experience for all of us. Our room in the hotel that was our headquarters in Taormina opened out onto a deck. There were orange trees loaded with ripe fruit below us, and there was a view of Mt. Etna, gently belching smoke and flames, near enough to add to the beauty of the night landscape but not near enough to be frightening. The one sad note came when a social-work administrator from New York, whom Grace had met on a sightseeing-bus trip around the island, gave us the news that David Rapaport, who had come to Boston for a visit before we flew for London in June, had died.

In the spring, Professor Nuttin invited both of us to give lectures at Louvain. The time we spent with him, as well as a call on Michotte, made this a memorable stay. After Louvain we were in Amsterdam, where we met several younger psychologists and had the special pleasure of a visit with Karl. He was still a graduate student at Harvard but was on his way to what was then Netherlands New Guinea to join a Harvard expedition headed by Robert Gardner for a summer of observation and photography in a village that had been known but not actually studied before. The other members of the group left at the end of the summer, but Karl stayed on for two years, broken only by a single visit to America, one might say as the only twentieth-century man in a Stone Age village.

In the summer I gave a lecture at Munich, where I had so long before spent a semester as a student, and was amused to find that I had to make use of a German dictionary when it came to some of the technical psychological terms I wanted to use, for there were some that had only come into my vocabulary during my life as an American psychologist. To anticipate, when I was to give a talk at Bielefeld some years later, a young Viennese social psychologist, Werner Herkner, read what I had written and made a few corrections in my German word order that must have slipped a little in the direction of English over the years.

Later in the spring came a visit from Roger and Louise Barker and their younger daughter, Lucy, and an amazingly beautiful trip by train from Oslo, in the southeastern part of Norway, to Trondheim, further north on the west coast. We took a mail boat along the fjords south to Bergen, a beautiful old port, largely rebuilt after the destruction of the war. The Barkers sailed from Bergen to England, where they were working on a study of a village in terms of their "ecological psychology"; and we returned to Oslo, again by train. We also went to Stockholm, sometimes called the Venice of the North because of its many canals, and spent an evening with a sociologist whom we had become acquainted with when he visited Oslo while we were there. A remark of his gives

180

one a feeling for the beauty of the Scandinavian summer. He had been a visiting professor in America for several years, and he spoke about an offer of a permanent position in an American university, which he had declined. We asked, out of real interest, why he had not accepted it. He thought for a moment, then said, almost as if he had never fully formulated it before, "I don't think I could live in a country that doesn't have the long summer days." Indeed, we realized, after our two summers there, how we loved the long daylight, the freedom to start on a walk or, less romantically, to hang out laundry, at almost any hour we pleased. The sudden darkness that closed in on us in Kansas seemed very arbitrary and annoying when we returned. In Oslo there were said to be a couple of hours of darkness on summer nights, but we never sat up late enough to see them. Winter in the city also had its own magic quality, when street lights and the lights of cars gave a soft glow through the darkness to the foggy sky and the snow under foot. More than that, we liked the winter climate, where the Gulf Stream kept the temperatures milder than the really cold spells of Kansas and made for a gradual drop to the winter cold and a gradual rise to the mild summer warmth, which was in happy contrast to the uncertain ups and downs that we had always known before.

We came back to America late in the summer, and I remember the hours that we spent playing Scrabble with Herbert and Rose Kelman as we crossed the Atlantic together by ship. They were two of the visiting Americans whom we had come to know best during that year in Oslo. Harold and Elsa Israel from our Smith College days were also fellow passengers. It was our last visit with Harold before he died of the heart trouble that had plagued him for several years.

Back in Lawrence I began teaching again at the university, and Grace, tired of commuting to Topeka, worked with me on a research project and at the same time busied herself finding a new place to live. Now that all three sons were away, except for visits, the large house of our first years in Kansas seemed rather too much. Grace found a house, closer to the campus, in which we saw possibilities. Its smaller rooms were more suited to our needs when we were alone, but it had sleeping space for everyone in the gradually expanding family. After a good deal of restoring and re-modeling, it gave us what we had especially wanted, a house that opened out onto a garden so that the two were almost a single unit. The Victorian house rather turned away from its out of doors.

The next year we were away again, this time at Duke University in Durham, North Carolina, where Donald Adams and Karl Zener, who had been in Berlin during my days there, were leading members of the Psychology Depart-ment. We had seen them regularly at meetings of the Lewin group in this country, and we remembered them especially from that first meeting in Northampton, just before New Year's Day, 1934. The temperatures had dropped to an unusual 30° below zero, and these two, from a more southern region where clothing was hardly planned for real cold, went about with all the extra wraps that we could borrow for them, so thoroughly swathed that they were known as the "invisible men" after the title of a popular moving picture of the day.

Our son John, who had tried a business career after he graduated from Harvard, had just that summer decided to become a psychologist and entered graduate school at Duke. He obtained his doctorate there and went on to become active in the encounter-group movement. Stephan, at the last moment, decided to stay with us and take a year of undergraduate work there. Fortunately, the house that we had taken for the academic year had space for all of us and for Karl, whose break in his New Guinea time came during that winter.

In the fall of 1963 I was again teaching in Kansas. In 1965 I received the Distinguished Scientific Contribution Award of the American Psychological Association and was especially pleased because our old friend, James Gibson, who had the task of presenting the awards that year, spoke of my "trailblazing thoughts about the fundamentals of perception" and said that I had shown "long ago the puzzle of the relations of things to their stimuli." I took that to mean that he had at least partly accepted the contention in my "Thing and Medium" that it is important for psychology to consider the "ecological" conditions of perception. Gibson died in 1979, and I regret that we had only rarely met in recent times to go on with the discussions of problems that had concerned both of us since we were together at Smith College.

I continued teaching until 1966, when I reached the age of seventy and, according to the rulings of the Board of Regents, was required to retire. In the meantime, the board had dropped its nepotism restrictions, and Beatrice Wright and Grace had become active members of the department. Beatrice had published her own important work entitled *Physical Disability: A Psychological Approach* in 1960 after helping me edit my book. Her book was already being used as a text by other members of the department before she was allowed to teach.

I had enjoyed my years of teaching, especially the close contact with graduate students whose master's theses and doctoral dissertations developed ideas with which I had worked over the years. Here I especially want to mention Nehemiah Jordan, whose dissertation dealt with "balance theory" and who has continued in his own energetic way to explore basic psychological and now philosophical ideas. But in spite of the satisfaction of teaching, I am glad to be free to devote myself to new ideas that come to me. All through the years I have been making notes about problems that I am trying to think through. I always have a little sheet of paper and a pencil stub in my pocket during the day and beside my bed at night, so as to be able to jot these thoughts down right away—otherwise they often seem to fade and get lost. Once

183

recorded, they are safe and I expand upon them, classify them to some extent, and copy them into notebooks. Actually, the book on interpersonal relations grew out of notes that I had made in this way and that I finally got time and help to put together properly. With the book completed, I began a new collection. Some of these have appeared in papers that I wrote over the next years, and many more repose in perhaps fifteen large loose-leaf notebooks that stand on a shelf in my Lawrence study.

Grace retired a little before the mandatory age so that we could travel to escape the chill of Kansas winters. We spent one academic quarter near the University of California at Los Angeles, when Karl was teaching there for a year, and we attended the seminar taught by Harold Kelley and Bernard Weiner on topics related to my work. Another year we were near Palo Alto, where we could see Karl and could also visit with John and his family in Mendocino. The next year we followed Karl to Columbia, South Carolina, where he had become chairman of the Department of Anthropology and where he now lives with his wife and children.

After Karl's first year in Columbia we began spending our winters in a condominium on an island near Grace's old home in Florida, where family could visit us and we could make detours to visit them—that is, the Columbia group. In the meantime *The Psychology of Interpersonal Relations* has continued to have repercussions that have been gratifying to me. To mention just a little of its recent impact, there are three volumes now in print by John H. Harvey and his colleagues William Ickes and Robert F. Kidd entitled *New Directions in Attribution Theory*, the first volume prefaced by an interview with Grace and me that the three editors made in Kansas, and in addition there have been conferences and reviews of work that develop ideas from the book. At the same time it gives me pleasure to know that Bernard Weiner and Marijana Benesh-Weiner, friends since our Los Angeles visit, have begun the task of dealing with material that is collected in my notebooks and that they are finding it something that has meaning for themselves and others.

And to round this narrative off—I am now the last member of my own generation from the large, spreading family that used to gather at the home in Feistritz—that is, the last except for my two half sisters, who in age belong more to the generation of my cousins' children than to mine. The old house has been sold, for there was nobody in the family who wanted to spend time there and be responsible for it, as the three women of my childhood had done—that is, my mother, Uncle Karl's wife, and my father's sister, Jetti; then Doris; and after her death, Gusti. My share of the proceeds were put into a Vienna bank for me. I learned that if I took the money out of the country, I would have to pay a considerable inheritance tax on it. So, we used it for several trips to Austria during the seventies, one including Stephan when he completed the work for his doctorate in physics. On each trip we saw the younger of my two half sisters, Gertraud, a physician who lives with her physician husband and one or two nearly grown children in the house that my father built for his young wife in the 1920s. And on what will probably prove to have been my last trip, in 1977, we were with two other younger members of the family whom we had last seen on our 1932 visit when they were probably six years old. One is Reingard, the elder of my half sisters, the first professional artist in a family whose members have carried sketchbooks and made watercolor and oil paintings over the generations; and the other is Tommi Reininghaus, the youngest son of my cousin Lilly. He brought two nearly grown children to have dinner with us at the hotel in Vienna where we spent the night before we flew home. And now, as perhaps a final event linking the series of happenings that have brought me from Austria to my American life, I may mention the honorary doctorate that was conferred on me through the Austrian Embassy in Washington, soon after my eighty-fifth birthday, by the University of Graz, where I received my original doctorate sixty-one years before.

Fritz Heider, in his study, 1981

As I bring this story of my eighty-five years to an end, I want to add a few thoughts about the changes that have come with my retirement fifteen years ago. I might more nearly have taken this for granted as just one more step in a routine life pattern if I had not been receiving questionnaires from scattered psychologists asking what retirement and aging involve both professionally and personally. I confess that I have not responded to most of these requests, as it would have diverted a slow-working person like me too

186

much from my two main goals, the completion of this narrative and the work that I want to do on my accumulated notes. But these questionnaires have made me think more specifically about what retirement may mean in general and about what it has meant in my own case. I have come to understand more and more the importance of what is really very simple, a truism—namely, that the meaning of aging and retirement depends on the effect they have on the day-by-day activities of the person concerned. If somebody has to stop doing what has given him a feeling of pride and self-fulfillment, then aging and retirement will be of great importance. It will be so for many who have worked all their lives as parts of larger establishments and whose jobs have involved the use of complicated apparatus or a role in networks of people.

But the activities that were most important to me were to a high degree independent of external equipment and resources, and of other people except as understanding friends and readers found some of my ideas useful in their own thinking and as they encouraged me to continue on my way. The activities that have meant most to me were centered on puzzling out problems in the theory of psychology, and most often they have consisted in attempts to bring greater clarity into the seeming confusion of commonsense notions.

It is true that I also loved teaching and discussions with students, but these have been added dividends, one might say. I did not really miss them after I retired, especially because we continued to live in an academic community, in which there were always people who lived here or who came to visit with whom I could talk, or people whom I saw when we traveled, especially during these last years, when Solomon Asch and Florence, from out of our past, have shared our Florida winters, as well as new acquaintances who have played their own important parts.

And there is no denying the fact that most of us have less available energy as we get older. At eighty-five I cannot

187

work as many hours a day as I could forty years, or even ten years, ago; and to be able to set my own schedule instead of building it around prescribed hours of a teaching program is a great boon.

Thus, since the activity that is central to me hardly changed after my retirement except as it was gradually reduced in the time I could spend on it each day, retirement has been of little importance in my life. I might add that the friendliness of our colleagues in the Psychology Department has made Grace and me feel very much part of what is happening there.

As I think about all this and look back over my life as a whole, I remember how Goethe once tried to describe in verse the fateful powers that guide our being. He gave them Greek names: the first he called "Daimon," by which he meant certain inborn tendencies, a constant direction of interest and actions that gives continuity to our existence and from which we can never escape. I suppose that different strands of Daimon existed in my own case, but the most lasting has simply been my theoretical interest in psychology. Partly this was a concern with perception and with the optical appearance of the environment, which was, of course, closely connected with the family's hobby of painting and sketching. At the same time, however, this interest was also directed toward a greater understanding of the engrossing relations between people. I felt the influence of both of these appeals very early in my childhood, and they still exert their influence over me.

Goethe called another power that rules our existence "Tyche," by which he meant our good or bad fortune, the influences from outside, which are exerted on us by the people and experiences that we encounter in the course of life. In thinking over the contingencies and eventualities of my life, I cannot help believing that it has been marked by many strokes of sheer luck. True enough, there have been troubling times, some bitter pills to be swallowed, but I am not sure whether in the end the anguish that I experienced was not beneficial, as I am pretty sure was the case with the difficulties I had as a boy before I entered the state gymnasium in Graz.

By now it seems to me that pieces of plain luck have been of decisive importance in many of the turning points in my life. I will mention a few examples. It was certainly sheer luck that these two professors, Meinong and Spitzer, were at the University of Graz, in the city in which I lived and would inevitably, in those difficult times, have spent most of my student years. The question from Meinong's book that started me toward the dissertation that I wrote for my doctorate and that influenced much of my thinking over the years would probably not have come to me with any other professor. And I am sure that there were very few professors in Germany or Austria who would have treated what I did with the understanding and encouragement that Meinong and Spitzer offered. Most of them would have objected to the absence of experimentation in the study. As to the theory of information transmission that I built from the question that intrigued me in Meinong's book, they would not have understood it and would have rejected the whole attempt. This positive response by the Graz people to my thesis is especially remarkable if one compares it to the relatively small effect that my papers on perception have had. A few people, as I have mentioned, have found them useful in their thinking, but it is my work on social relations that has become known these last years.

And later, when I was on my own, it was again luck that it was in Berlin that I had the possibility of staying with relatives and so came to know the men of the Berlin school of gestalt psychology, and also Lewin, who seemed to understand so quickly the direction in which I wanted to work.

Then, in that period of life, came Gusti's financial help, without which I might never have been able to pull myself together and find my way as a psychologist. But I believe that the most striking instance of good fortune was, without doubt, meeting Grace in the Research Department of the school for the deaf in Northampton. I shudder to think of all the factors related to this meeting that had to work in coordination to bring this about and how easily any one of them might have happened differently and thus caused the whole chain of events to move in a different direction. Some of these factors were decisions of my own in years long past which I made in what seems a perfectly haphazard way— haphazard certainly as regards this final outcome and their importance for my future life. For instance, if I had decided in 1927 to accept Bühler's offer of an assistantship in Vienna instead of Stern's for Hamburg, I would almost certainly never have been offered the position in Northampton with Koffka, and I would probably never have come to America.

Another happy event was being asked by Roger Barker whether I would consider coming to Kansas, just at the time when I most needed to make a change. That question brought us to this haven where we have made our home for thirty-some years and where our three sons grew up so comfortably. There were many more such turning points in this story that came at exactly the right moment to produce the end effect that seems so happy when I put it all together. As a matter of fact, if I were inclined to be superstitious, I could believe that a friendly spirit arranged the whole sequence of events in which the powers of fortune were so kind to me.

Index